Better Homes and Gardens®

NEW
EDITION

grandma's best
full-size quilt blocks

Meredith Books®
Des Moines, Iowa

NEW EDITION
grandma's best
full-size quilt blocks

Contributing Editor: Carol Field Dahlstrom
Contributing Graphic Designer: Angie Haupert Hoogensen
Copy Chief: Terri Fredrickson
Publishing Operations Manager: Karen Schirm
Senior Editor, Asset & Information Management:
 Phillip Morgan
Edit and Design Production Coordinator: Mary Lee Gavin
Editorial Assistant: Kaye Chabot
Book Production Managers: Pam Kvitne,
 Marjorie J. Schenkelberg, Rick von Holdt, Mark Weaver
Contributing Copy Editor: Mary Helen Schiltz
Contributing Proofreader: Mindy Kralicek
Contributing Photographers: Bill Hopkins, Scott Little,
 Andy Lyons Cameraworks
Contributing Technical Illustrator: Chris Neubauer
Contributing Stitchers: Dawn Cavanaugh, Sherie Johnson,
 JoAnn Olson, Margaret Sindelar, Pat Taylor, Jan Temeyer

Meredith® Books
Executive Director, Editorial: Gregory H. Kayko
Executive Director, Design: Matt Strelecki
Managing Editor: Amy Tincher-Durik
Senior Editor/Group Manager: Vicki Leigh Ingham
Marketing Product Manager: Toye Cody

Publisher and Editor in Chief: James D. Blume
Editorial Director: Linda Raglan Cunningham
Executive Director, New Business Development:
 Todd M. Davis
Executive Director, Sales: Ken Zagor
Director, Operations: George A. Susral
Director, Production: Douglas M. Johnston
Director, Marketing: Amy Nichols
Business Director: Jim Leonard

Vice President and General Manager: Douglas J. Guendel

Better Homes and Gardens® **Magazine**
Editor in Chief: Gayle Goodson Butler

Meredith Publishing Group
President: Jack Griffin
Senior Vice President: Karla Jeffries

Meredith Corporation
Chairman of the Board: William T. Kerr
President and Chief Executive Officer: Stephen M. Lacy

In Memoriam: E.T. Meredith III (1933–2003)

All of us at Meredith® Books are dedicated to providing
you with information and ideas to create beautiful and useful
projects. We welcome your comments and suggestions.
Write to us at: Meredith Books, Crafts Editorial Department,
1716 Locust Street—LN126, Des Moines, IA 50309-3023.

table *of* contents

stars & hearts

Simple motifs such as stars and hearts are the inspiration for many of the quilt patterns that continue to be favorites today. Quilt blocks such as Lone Star, Tipsy Star, Autumn Star, and Floral Heart are just a few of the patterns quilters have used for decades. In this chapter you'll find beautiful quilt blocks that reflect these favorite designs. PAGES **4-55**

pretty florals

Pieced floral blocks and elegant appliquéd flowers have always inspired quilters with their color, shape, and beauty. Wild Rose, Dogwood, Peony, and Texas Tulip, are some of the quilt blocks to pick from in this lovely chapter filled with pretty blooms. PAGES **56-105**

vintage classics

Quilt patterns such as Prairie Queen, Goosetracks, Drunkard's Path, and Dresden Plate bring images of finely stitched quilts of long ago. This chapter offers you block after block of these timeless classics in colors and variations for today's quilter. PAGES **106-159**

favorite geometrics

From Amish Cross and Turkey Tracks Variation to King's Crown and Streak of Lightning, beautifully basic geometrics capture the attention of quilters everywhere. Look for color choices and patterns that will inspire you to create a quilted masterpiece in geometrics. PAGES 160-205

borders & edgings

The finishing of a quilt is the added detail that sets it apart. Find the perfect border and edging pattern in this chapter to make your quilt one-of-a-kind. PAGES **206-213**

quilting basics PAGES **214-215**   index, sources & resources PAGE **216**

stars
&
hearts

*As women designed and stitched quilts for
their families, favorite motifs such as stars and
hearts found their way into these exquisite quilts.
These universal motifs, found in utilitarian
household objects as well, became common
shapes that quilters used again and again.*

INSPIRATION

Simple motifs are often the beginning of exquisite designs in quilting patterns. From the time that American women began making quilts, the simple shapes of the star and heart found their way into beautiful quilting patterns.

Star shapes are natural ones for quilters in many ways, because the corners of the patchwork often form stars with varying points. With slight variations, the same similar star pattern can take on a new look and a new name.

The Lone Star quilt block is likely one of the most recognizable star quilt patterns to Americans. It is also one of the oldest patterns. There are several variations with six, eight, and even more points. The same pattern can be called one thing in one part of the country and quite another elsewhere. Mathematical Star was an early name used along the Eastern seaboard, especially near Baltimore. The Star of Bethlehem was a well-known name for it all across the

country and is still used today. Other names include Star of the East, and Morning Star.

The same star pattern when made much smaller so that many cover the surface is known by other names such as Blazing Star; when the points touch it is called Touching Star. When a large Lone Star is placed inside of a curved set of similar diamond-shape blocks that encircle it and form a half-star, it is called a Broken Star.

Quilt block star patterns can be found by the dozens, including Star and Crescent, Star and Chains, Rainbow Star, Star Puzzle, Twinkling Stars, Royal Star, and Ohio Star, to name just a few.

Heart motifs have been used again and again, both in patchwork and appliqué. Floral heart wreaths were favorites, as were center heart block patterns. To manage the curve of a pieced heart indicates the talent and patience of the quilter.

The shape of the heart is classic. Hearts and Gizzards, a favorite vintage pattern with an unforgettable name, forms the heart using two different colors. The blocks can be set together to form new shapes or separately, creating unique round shapes. Hearts and Spades is another pattern from the mid 1800s as is Hearts and Tulips.

ABOVE *Beautiful cut and pressed glassware from the 1800s and early 1900s often featured etched stars in the glass design. Stars appeared in many quilt designs during this period.*

The versatility of the ever-popular star and heart shapes inspire quilters to use these images over and over again in their pieced and appliqué quilts.

LEFT *Hearts were such a popular motif in the early 1900s that utilitarian kitchen items such as waffle irons even repeated the design.*
RIGHT *Cookie cutters and other simple motifs reflected in daily life may have been some inspiration for quilt blocks.*

silk stars

HOW TO CONSTRUCT THIS BLOCK

Sew A to A (4 times). Stitch two AA together (2 times). Sew the two units together. Sew B to B (2 times). Stitch two BB together. Machine-appliqué the star in place, matching the points with the background seam lines. Use matching threads to appliqué.

HOW TO MAKE THIS QUILT

This quilt is designed to be a full-size quilt measuring 90×90 inches, including 4½-inch-wide sashing strips with setting squares and 9-inch-wide borders with corner Star blocks.

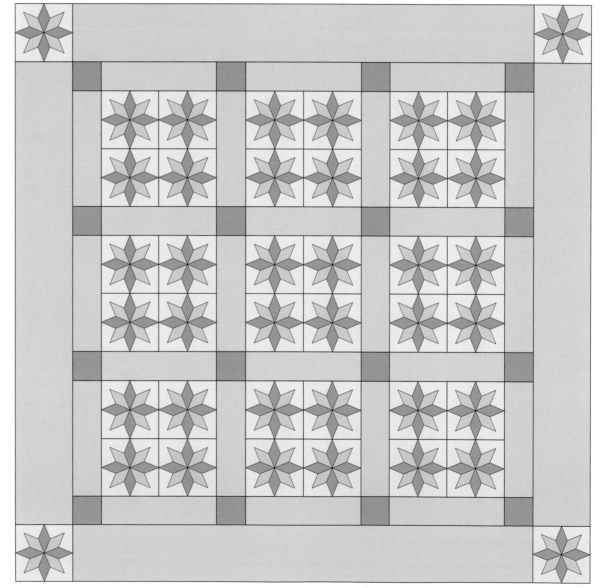

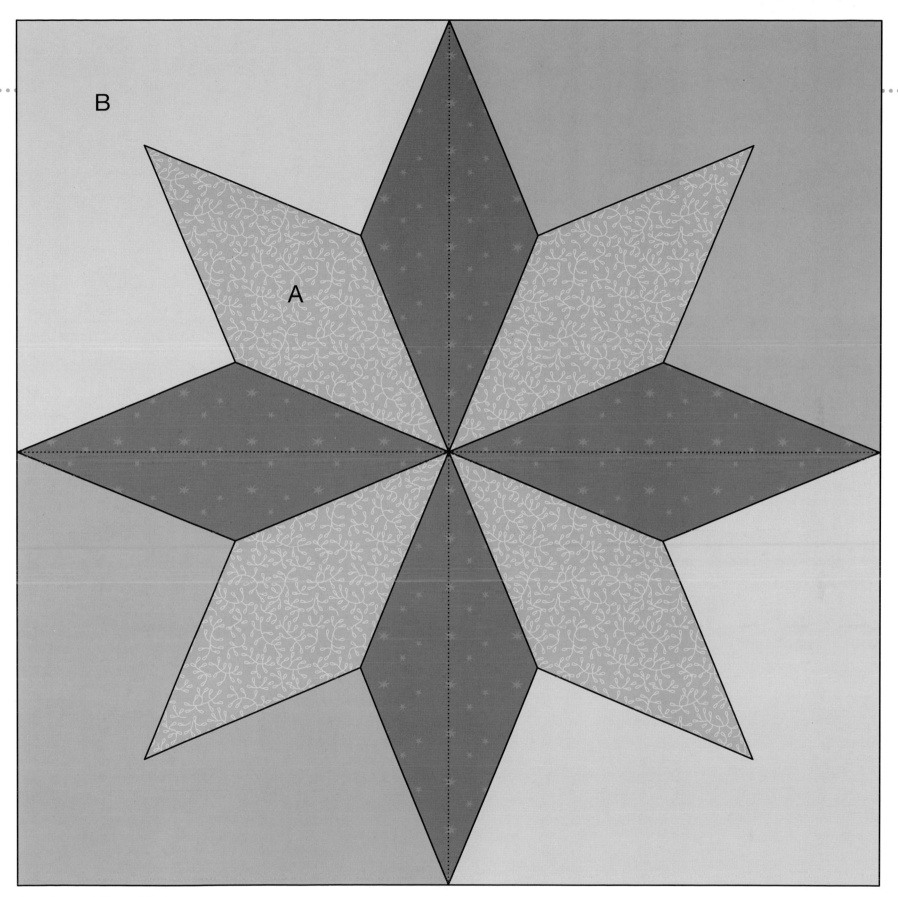

B

A

SILK STARS *full-size block*

dimensional star

HOW TO CONSTRUCT THIS BLOCK

Make 4 A sections by joining pieces in numerical order. Make 4 B sections and join each to an A section. Make 4 C sections; then 4 D sections and join each C section to a D section. Join each A B unit to a C D unit. Repeat to make a total of 4 A B C D units. Join the 4 units to complete the block.

look again

When this block is set together in fours, the dark and light fabrics create a new star in the middle forming a square center with radiating triangles.

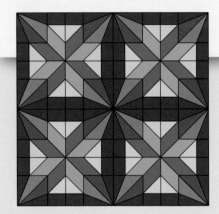

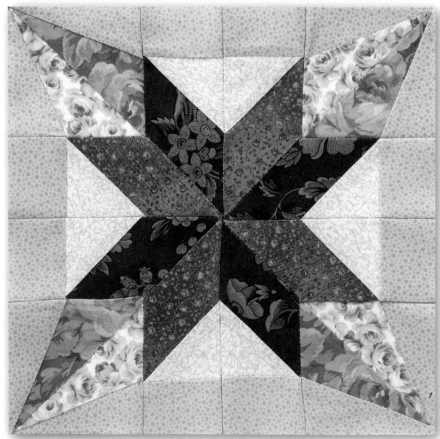

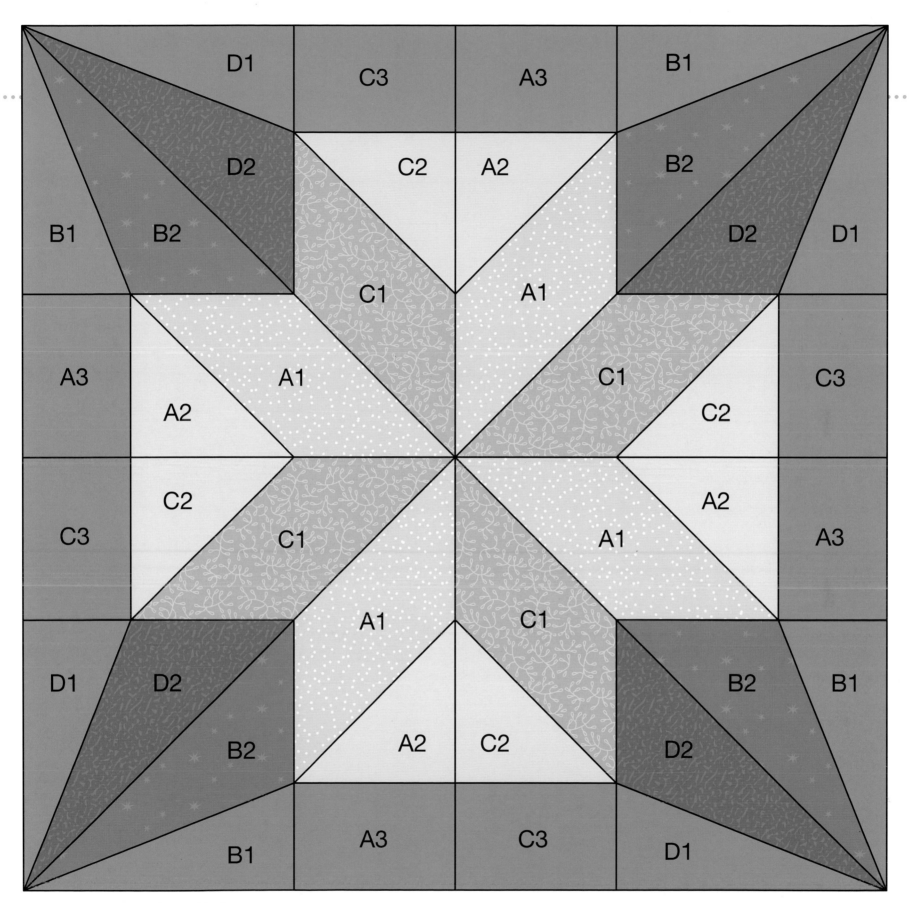

DIMENSIONAL STAR *full-size block*

mosaic star

HOW TO CONSTRUCT THIS BLOCK

Lay out pieces in correct positions, noting placement of half-square triangles for each CC unit. Sew A to Ar (4 times). Sew one long edge of C to A (4 times). Sew one long edge of C to Ar (4 times). Set in B to AArCC (4 times). Stop the stitching at the seam line of AAr. Reposition B and begin stitching at the seam line, being careful not to stitch through the AAr seam line. Sew two AArBC together (2 times). Stitch the two units together to form a center star.

Join C to C (24 times). Horizontally sew each row together. For Row 1 and Row 8: Stitch two Bs, four CC units, two Bs. For Row 2 and Row 7: Stitch three Bs, two CC units, three Bs. For Row 3 and Row 6: Stitch separate row units of one CC unit and one B unit (4 times). For Row 4 and Row 5: Stitch two separate row units of two CC units each.

Sew one Row 3 unit to one Row 4 unit (2 times). Sew one Row 5 unit to one Row 6 unit (2 times). Sew the Row 3, 4 unit to the Row 5, 6 unit (2 times). Stitch one Row 3, 4, 5, 6 to the left side of the star center and one to the right side of the star center. Stitch Row 1 to Row 2; join to the top of the star center. Stitch Row 7 to Row 8; join to the bottom of the star center.

HOW TO MAKE THIS QUILT

This quilt is designed to be a twin-size quilt measuring 72×90 inches. Four rows of triangle squares form the border, with stars from the center of the block set in each corner.

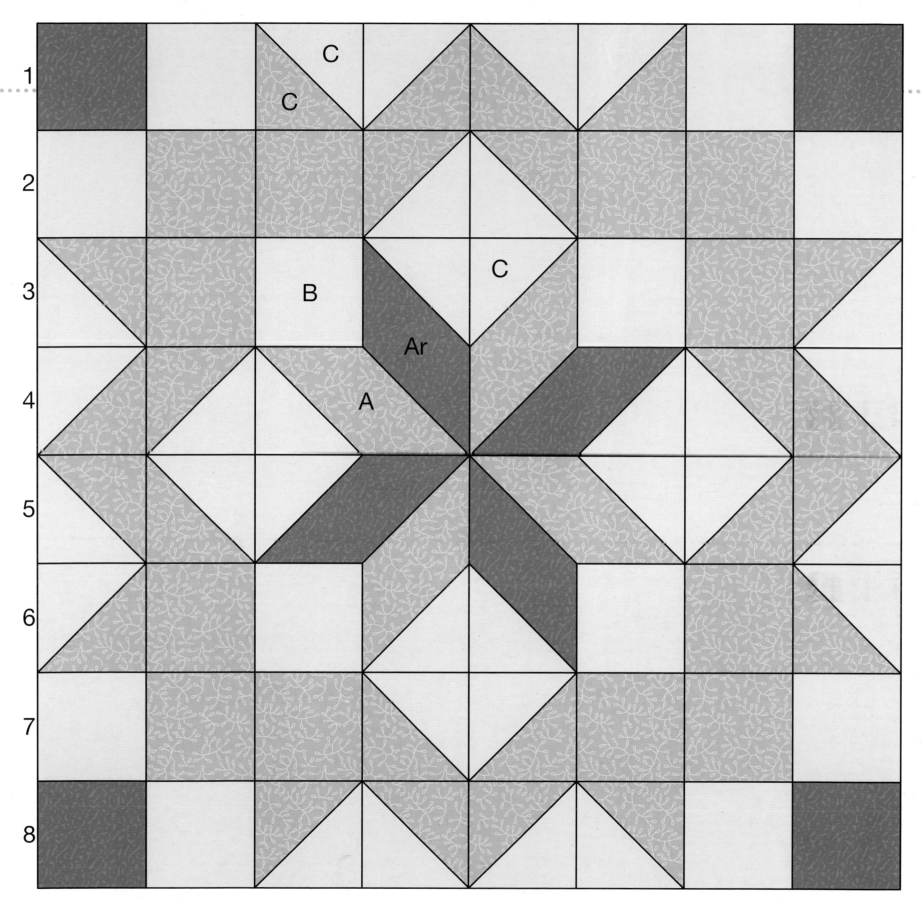

Mosaic Star *full-size block*

star fan

HOW TO CONSTRUCT THIS BLOCK

Trace fan placement onto 9½-inch square background fabric. Cut seven 2½-inch squares for prairie points. To make prairie points, press square in half diagonally with wrong sides facing to form a triangle. Press triangle in half matching raw edges. Baste prairie points to background fabric indicated by the dashed-and-dotted line on pattern, with ¼-inch seam. Press under seam allowance at top edge of all As. Baste A to background fabric at bottom edge of block. With right sides facing, stitch A to basted A. Press to right side. Continue stitching and pressing A to A (5 times) to complete fan. Appliqué top edge of fan over prairie point raw edges. Machine-baste block edges as needed. Appliqué B and C to background fabric. Detail fan and star with the blanket stitch if desired.

HOW TO MAKE THIS QUILT

This quilt is designed to be a twin square quilt measuring 81×81 inches. A 4½-inch solid border with an appliquéd star in the corner border blocks is shown.

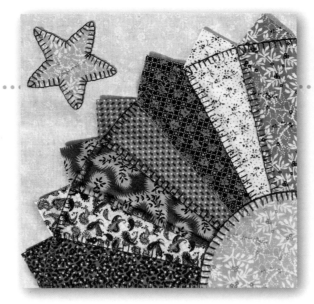

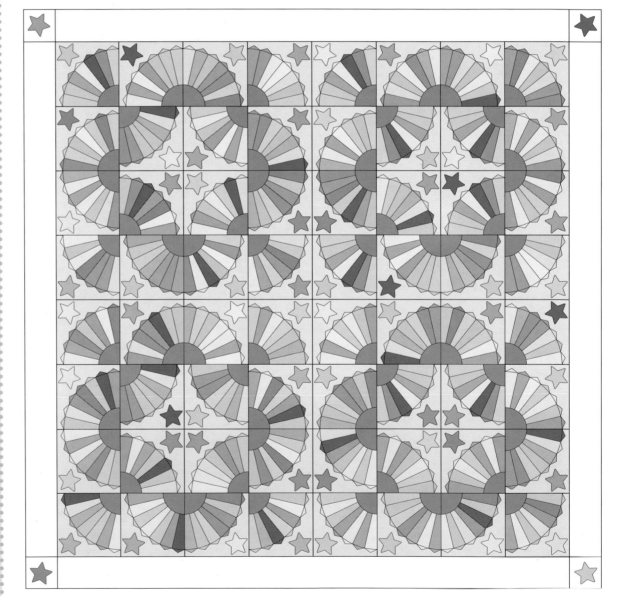

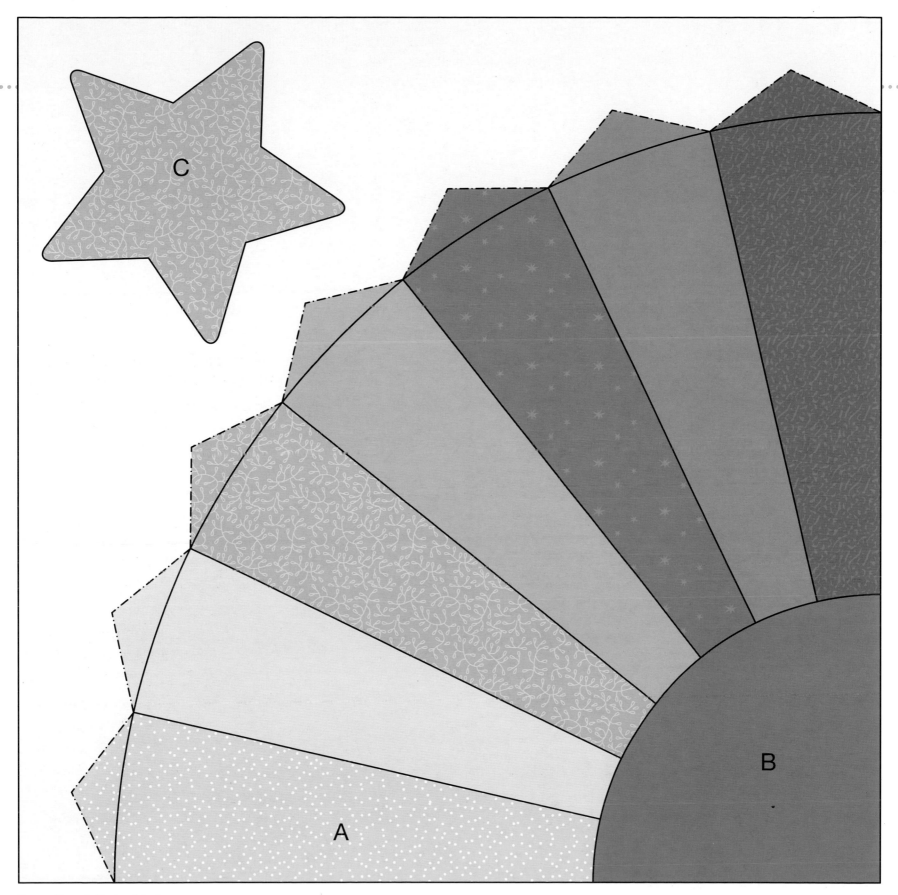

STAR FAN *full-size block*

mariner's compass

HOW TO CONSTRUCT THIS BLOCK

Join C to D, join Cr to E; sew CD to CrE; add B, then A. Make 4 units (called A units). Sew Cr to Dr, sew C to Er; join CrDr to CEr; add Br, then Ar. Make 4 units (called Ar units). Join A units to Ar units along the B edges (4 times). Sew resulting square units together in 2 rows, then join rows to make the block.

about this block

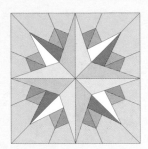

This vintage star pattern, Mariner's Compass, has been a classic for almost 200 years. The star design that radiates from the center is nicely complex and allows for the quilter to show off her remarkable piecing skills. The triangular pieces must be pieced with precision to yield the stunning outcome.

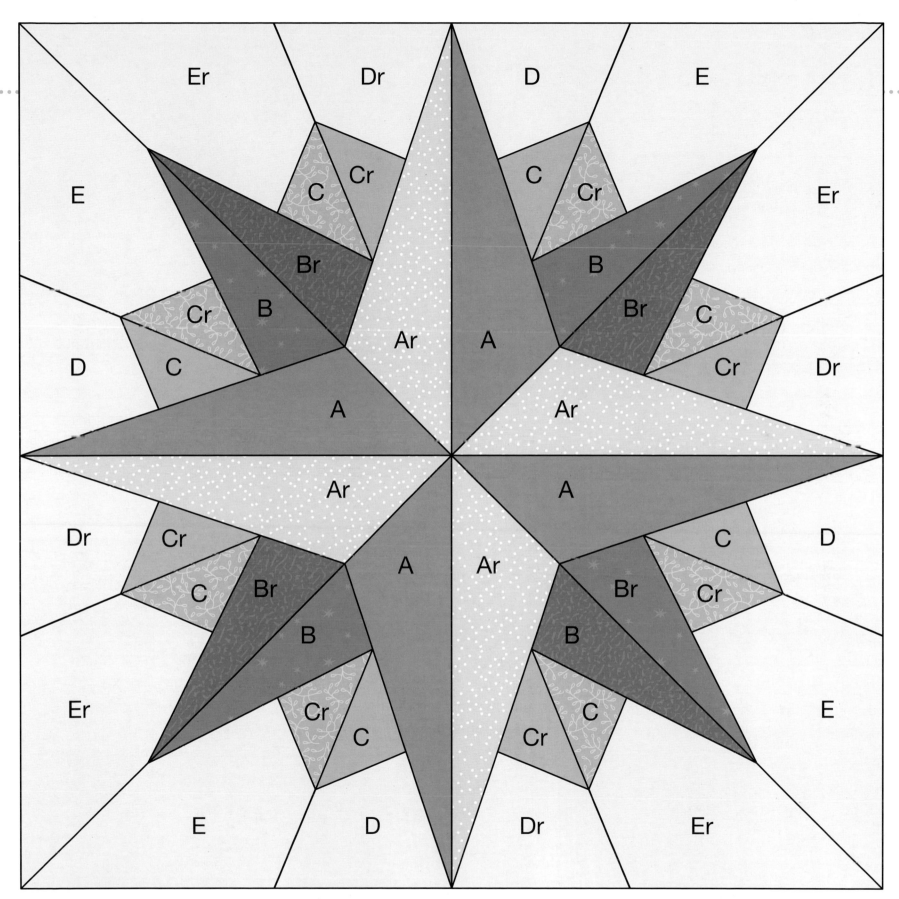

Mariner's Compass *full-size block*

tipsy star

HOW TO CONSTRUCT THIS BLOCK

Stitch B and Br (4 times). Set in C to BBr (4 times). Sew a BBrC unit to top and bottom of A. Join two Cs (4 times). Add CC to each side of BBrC unit (2 times). Sew CCBBrCCC to each side of BBrCABBC. Sew D to E (4 times). Sew C to E (4 times). Join DE to CE (4 times). Add DECE to each side of center unit.

HOW TO MAKE THIS QUILT

This quilt is designed to be a queen-size quilt measuring 91¾×104½ inches. The block is set on point with 9-inch setting sqaures between. A combination of 3-, 3-, 2-, 3-, and 3-inch-wide solid-color borders finishes the quilt as shown.

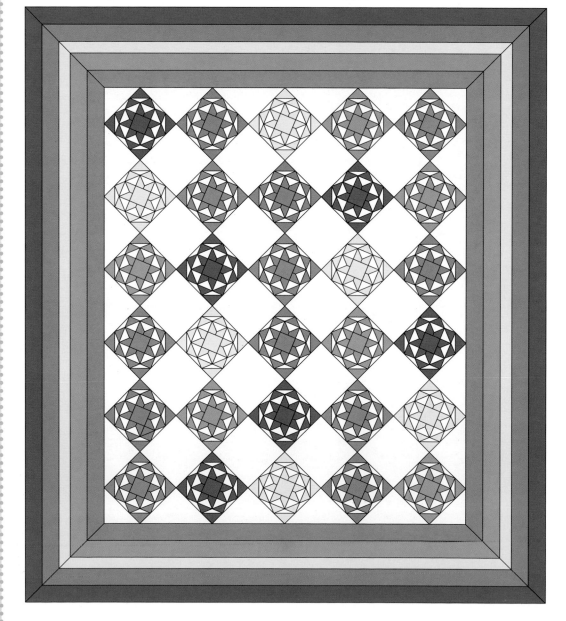

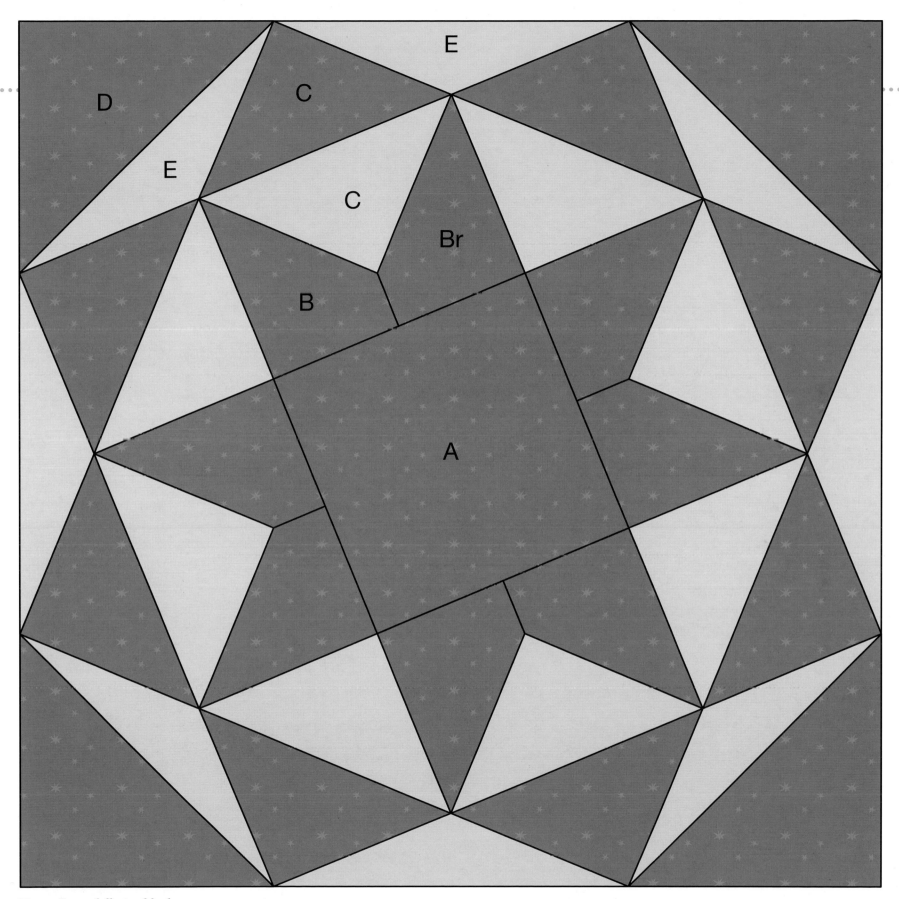

TIPSY STAR *full-size block*

floral heart

HOW TO CONSTRUCT THIS BLOCK

Appliqué hearts and flowers. Embroider the line that forms the heart with a favorite embroidery stitch such as the stem stitch (see page 214).

about this block

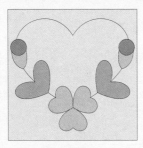

Embroidered quilt blocks have always been popular, but combining embroidery with appliqué offers no limit to the design of the block. In the Floral Heart block, bottom right, the stem stitch was used to make the heart with appliquéd hearts forming flower like petals. Use machine or hand embroidery to achieve the look you like.

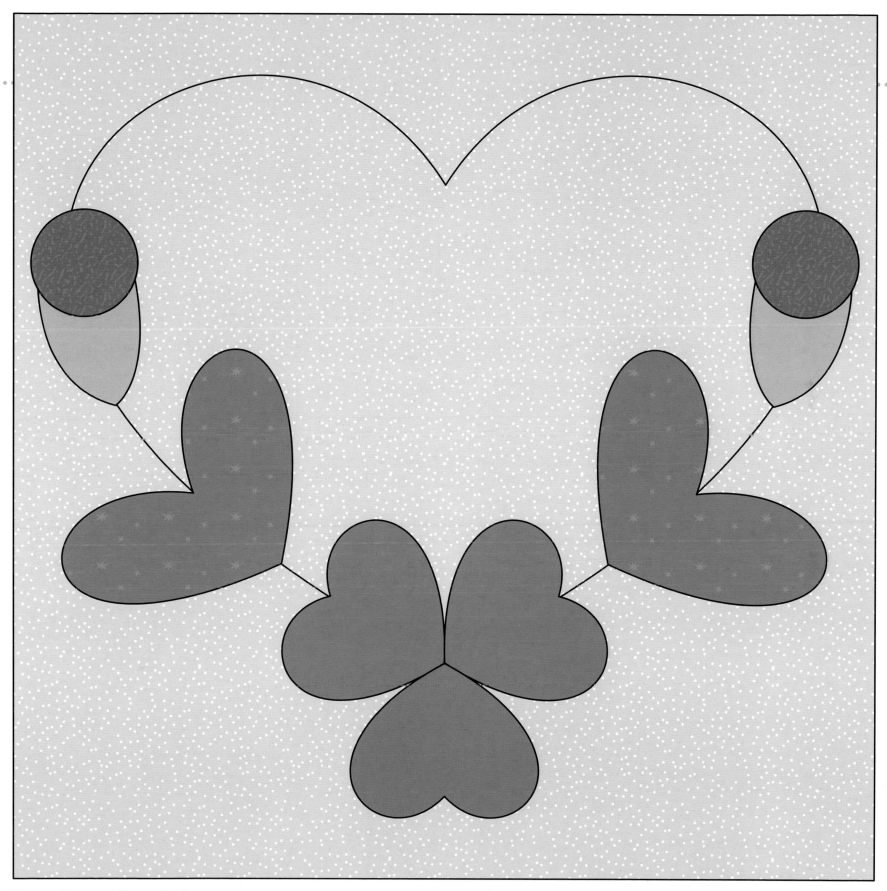

FLORAL HEART *full-size block*

lone star

HOW TO CONSTRUCT THIS BLOCK

Make CCCC unit as you would a Four-Patch (see page 214) to make each star point section (8 times). Sew the sections together in pairs, being careful not to sew in the seam allowances that will be mitered. Sew the pairs together to make two halves, then join the halves. Set in the A pieces (see page 215 for mitering directions), then set in the B pieces.

look again

This all-time favorite pattern can be put together into a quilt in so many different ways. Abutting the blocks together with no sashing yields an interesting square and diamond pattern between the stitched blocks.

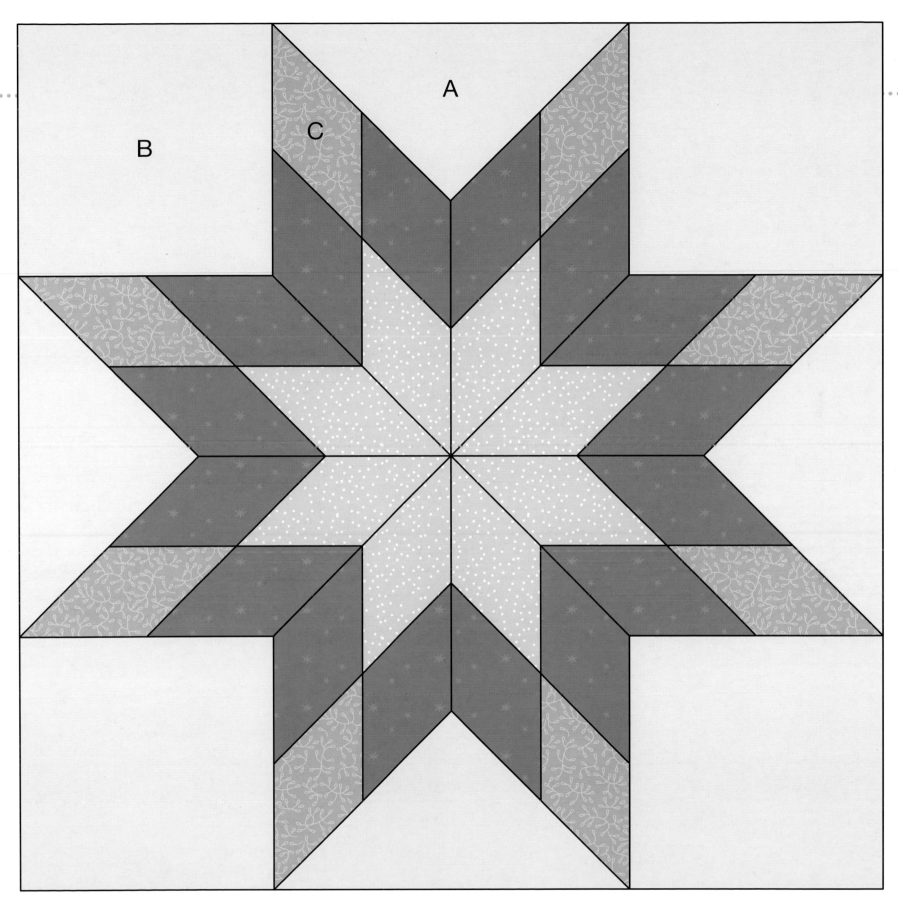

LONE STAR *full-size block*

geometric star

HOW TO CONSTRUCT THIS BLOCK

Make 2 A sections by joining the A pieces in numerical order. Make 2 B sections. Join an A section to a B section twice to make 2 A B units. Join the 2 units to complete the block.

look again

This star block pattern looks three-dimensional within the block itself, but when it is combined with three identical blocks, a new solid-color star pattern forms in the middle of each set of four.

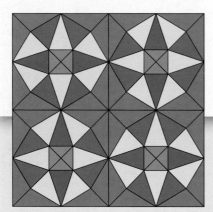

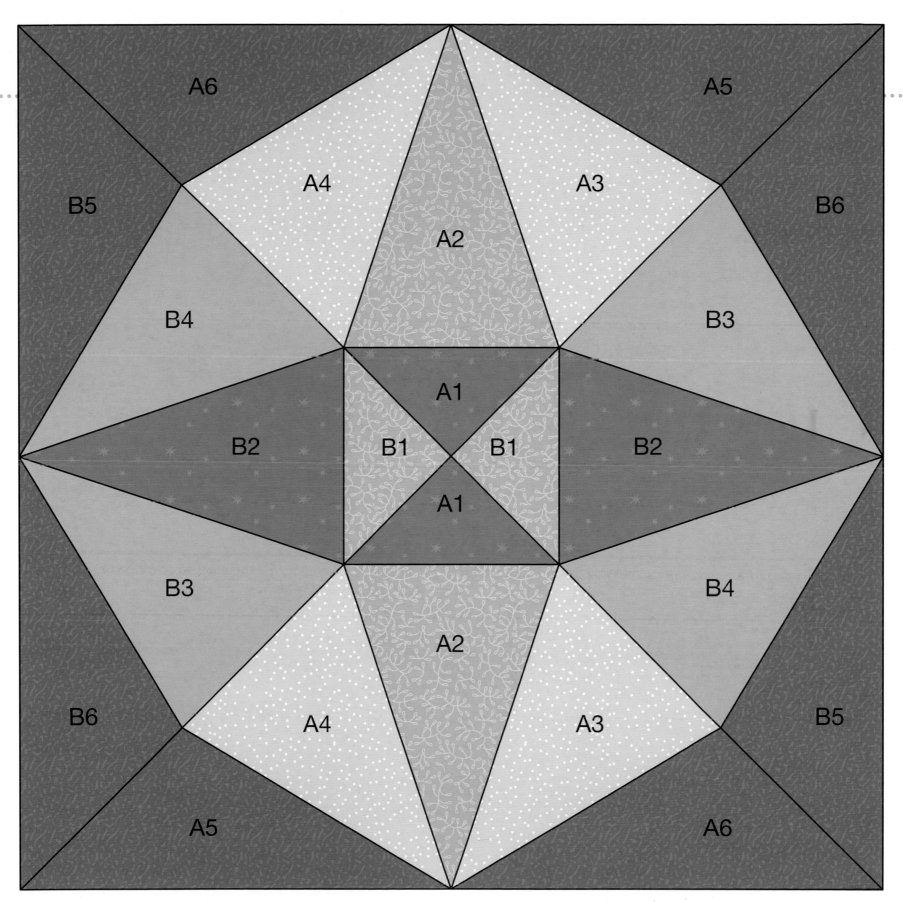

GEOMETRIC STAR *full-size block*

four stars

HOW TO CONSTRUCT THIS BLOCK

Unit 1: Sew B to A (8 times). Add B to the other side of A (8 times). Sew C to ABB (4 times). Sew ABB to outside edge of E (4 times). Add ABBC to adjoining outside edge of EABB to complete four of Unit 1.

Unit 2: To opposite sides of G, add F (8 times). To the remaining opposite sides of FFG, add F (8 times). Sew D to FFFFG (4 times) to complete four of Unit 2.

Horizontally sew each row together. Rows 1 and 3: Sew Unit 1, Unit 2, and Unit 1 together. Row 2: Sew Unit 2, E, and Unit 2 together. Stitch Row 1 to Row 2; add Row 3.

HOW TO MAKE THIS QUILT

This quilt is designed to be a full-size quilt measuring 90×90 inches, including 9-inch-wide pieced sashing strips with four nine-patch setting squares (composed of 3-inch squares). The mitered inner border is 6 inches wide, and the outer border measures 3 inches wide.

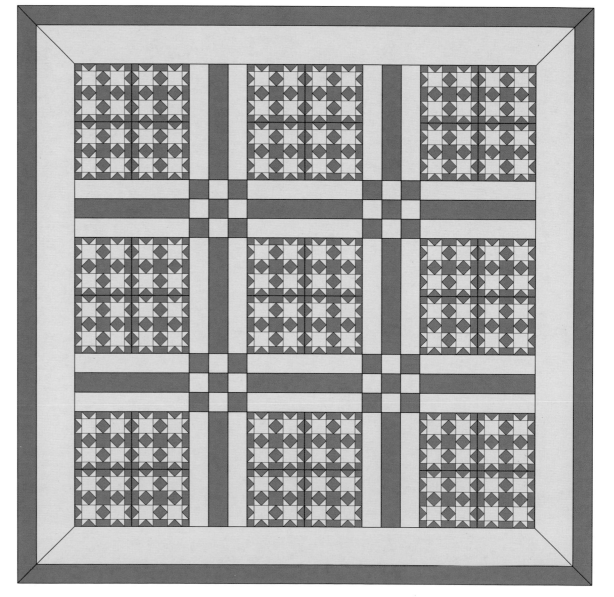

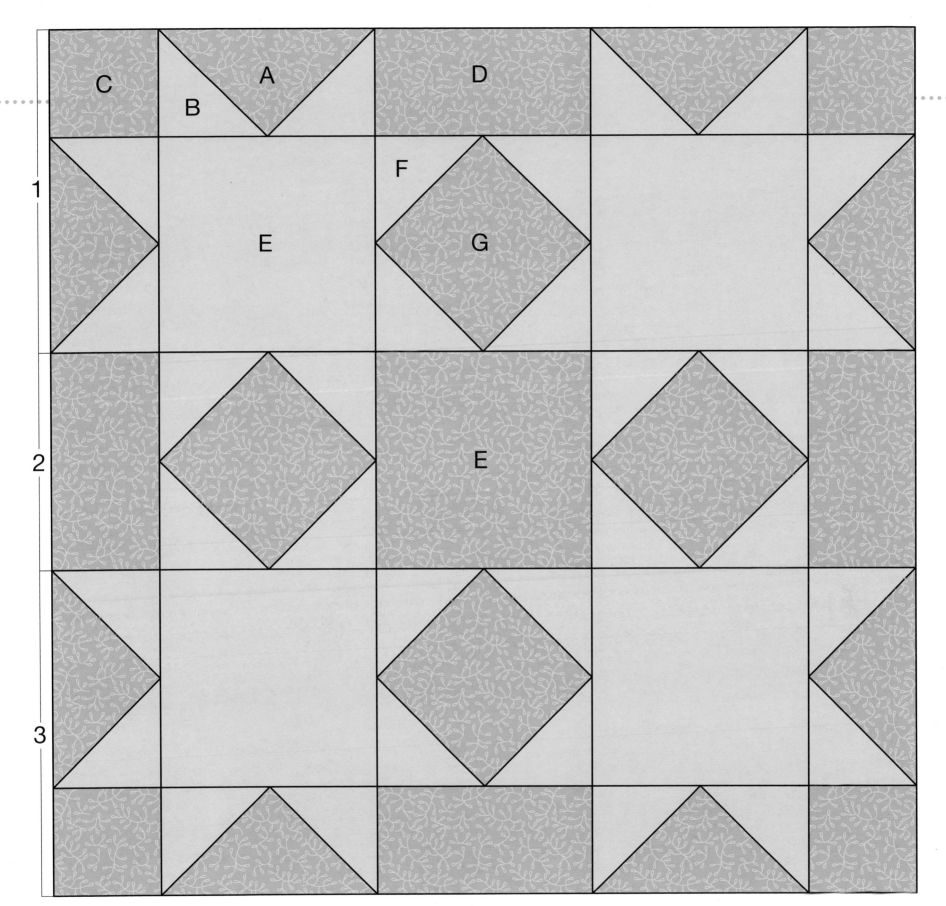

FOUR STARS *full-size block*

four-pointed checkered star

HOW TO CONSTRUCT THIS BLOCK

Make 4 A sections by joining the A pieces in numerical order. Make 2 B C units. Make 2 D E units. Make 1 F G unit. Assemble block in 3 rows. Make a B-C-A-D-E row, and A F G A row and a D E A B C row. Join the rows to complete the block.

look again

Four-Patch blocks in the corners on this star block form the central square that appears when the blocks are butted together creating the quilt. Managing the lights and darks of the squares is important to get the look you want in the finished quilt.

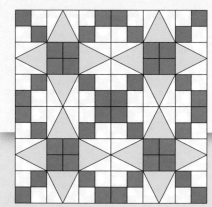

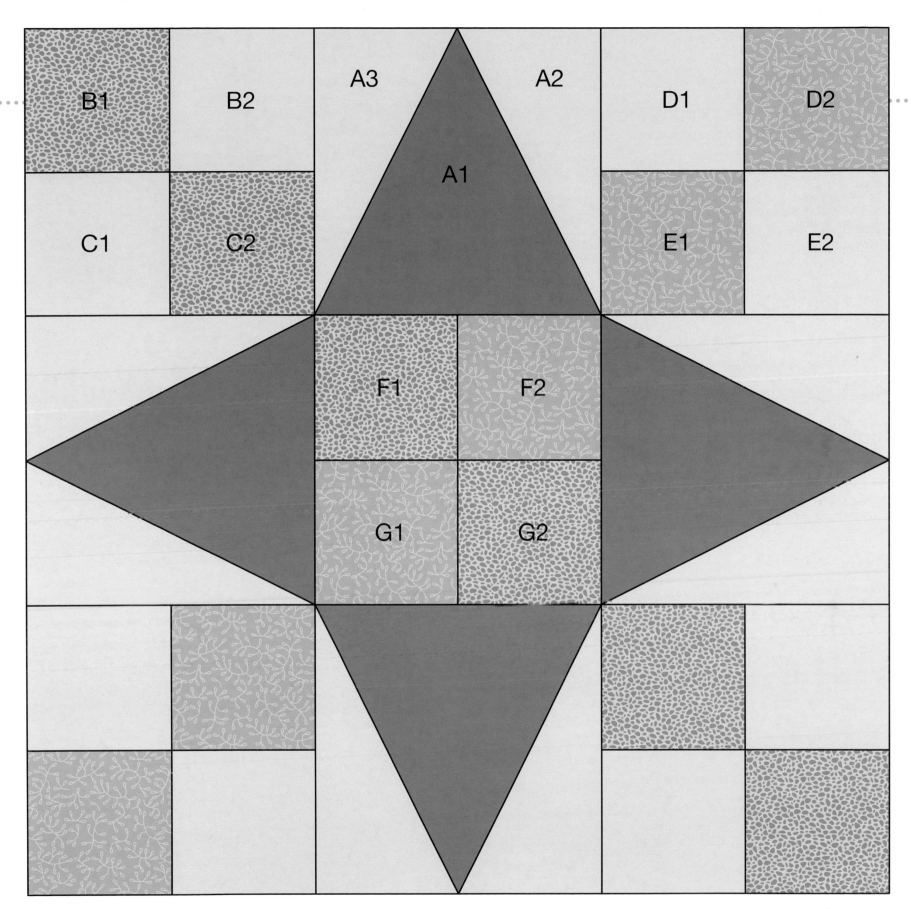

FOUR-POINTED CHECHERED STAR *full-size block*

four hearts

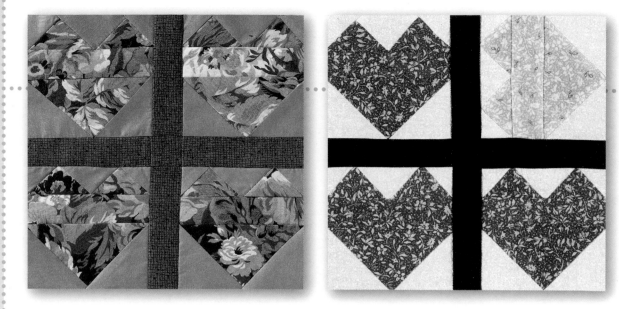

HOW TO CONSTRUCT THIS BLOCK

Sew A to B (8 times). Sew AB to A; add AB (4 times). Sew C to ABAAB (4 times). Sew E to D (4 times); add E (4 times). Sew EDE to ABAABC (4 times) to make heart. Sew G to edge of two hearts (2 times). Sew G to F; add G. Sew GFG between two sets of hearts. Rotate any heart unit 90 degrees as desired.

HOW TO MAKE THIS QUILT

This quilt is designed to be a twin-size quilt measuring 72×94 inches. It uses 2-inch-wide sashing strips, a 2-inch-wide solid border; a 10-inch-wide solid border, and a 3-inch-wide solid border as shown.

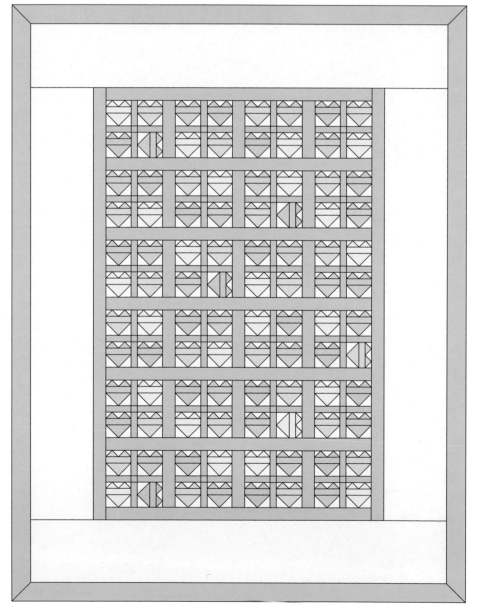

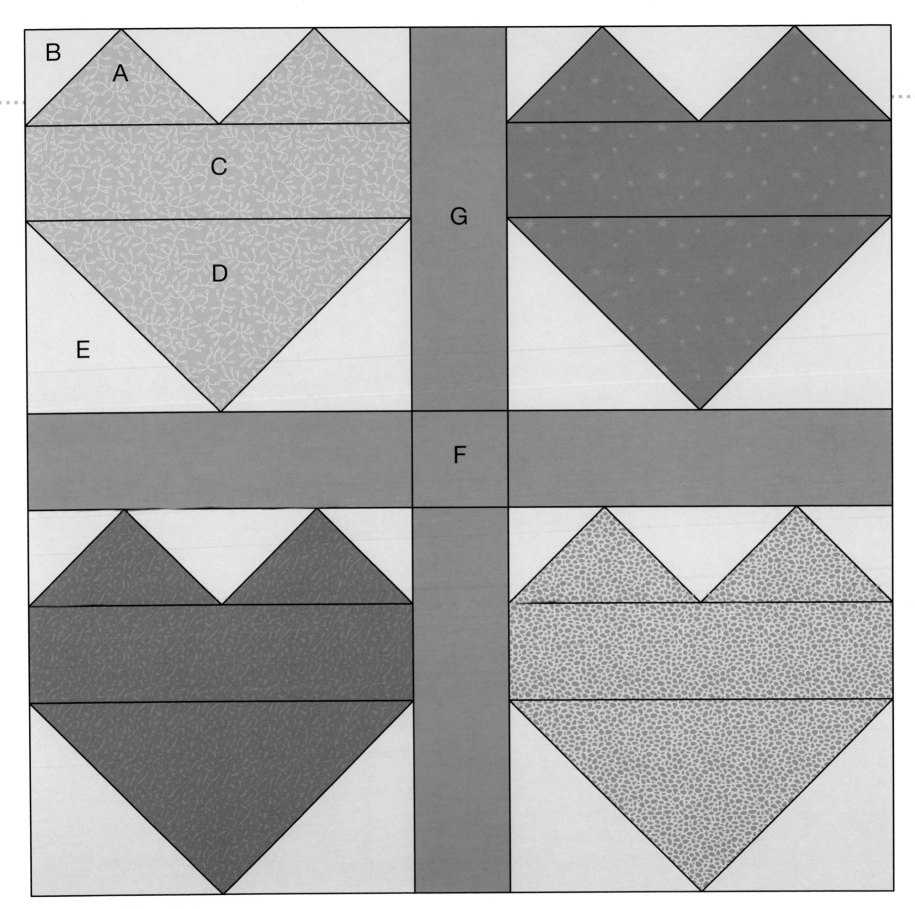

FOUR HEARTS *full-size block*

twisted star

HOW TO CONSTRUCT THIS BLOCK

Join A1, A2, and A3. Make 4 A sections. Join B1 and B2. Make 4 B sections. Join A and B sections to make 4 squares. Join the 4 A B units to complete the block.

about this block

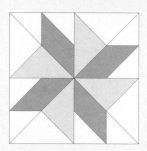

The star and its many variations are probably the most popular motifs in pieced quilts. Because of the very nature of piecing triangles and squares, star shapes appear almost like magic.

This pattern, a variation of the Ohio Star, uses long triangles to nudge the star out of its conventional, upright position. The combined blocks, slightly tipsy, add movement to the finished quilt.

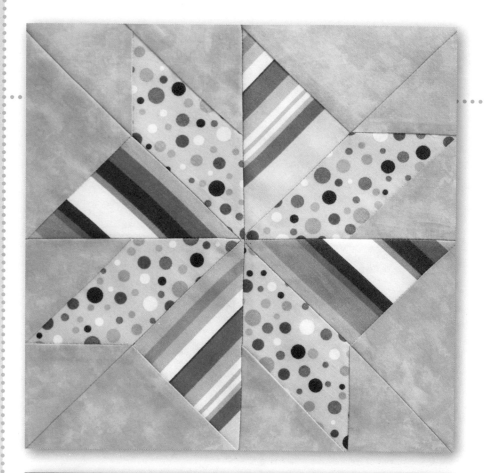

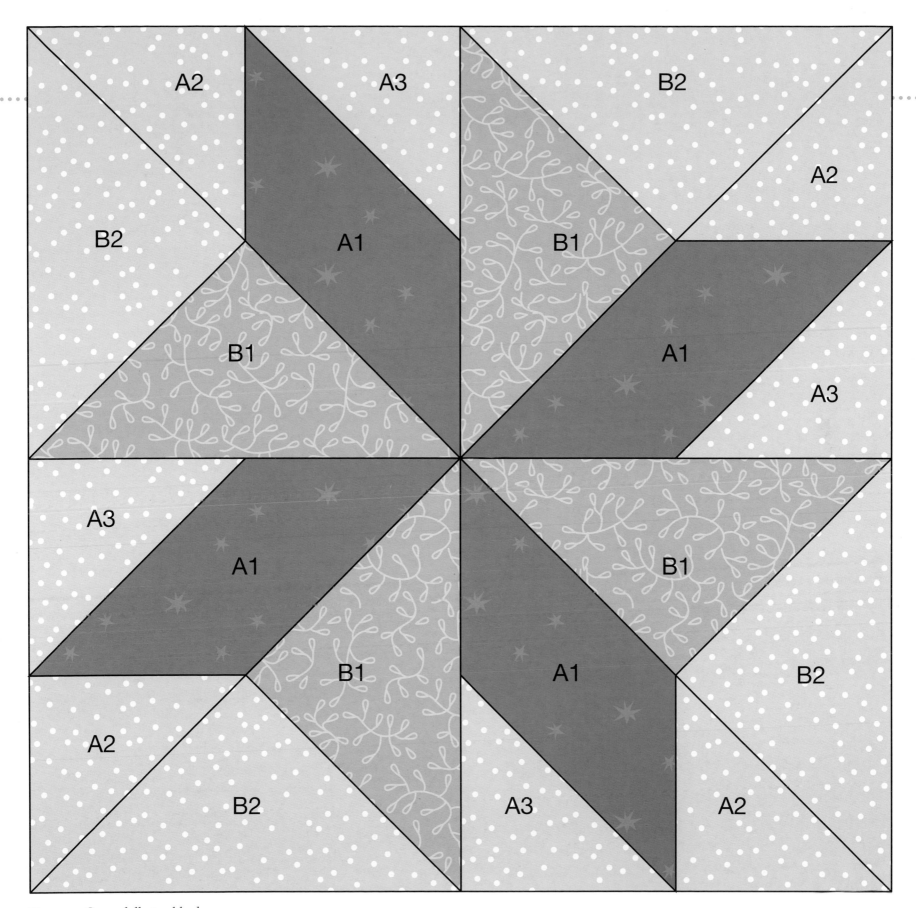

Twisted Star *full-size block*

two star

HOW TO CONSTRUCT THIS BLOCK

Star unit: Sew A to B (4 times); add B to AB (4 times). Sew B to each side of BAB (2 times). Sew BAB to opposite sides of C (2 times). Sew BBABB to opposite sides of BABCBAB. Repeat these steps for a second star unit. Stripe unit: Sew four Ds together (2 times). Sew star unit to stripe unit (2 times). Sew two sets together.

HOW TO MAKE THIS QUILT

This quilt is designed to be a twin-size quilt measuring 63×90 inches. It uses the 4½-inch-wide Triangles border, see page 208, as shown.

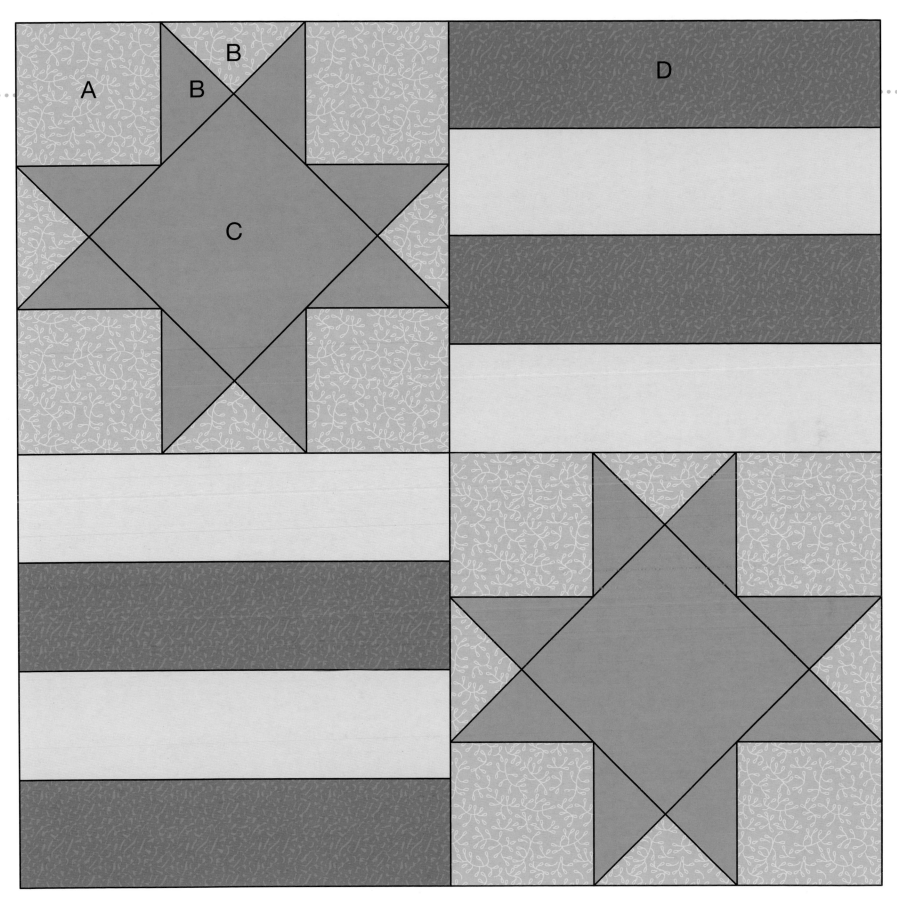

TWO STAR *full-size block*

autumn star

HOW TO CONSTRUCT THIS BLOCK

Make 2 A sections by joining the A pieces in numerical order. Join the 2 A sections. Make 4 B sections. Join 2 B sections to opposite sides of the A A unit. Join C1 pieces to opposite ends of 2 B sections. Join the C B C units to the top and bottom of the center B A B unit.

look again

A favorite block for generations, this block can be combined nicely with other star blocks. When sewn with no sashing, a beautiful geometric square forms in the middle.

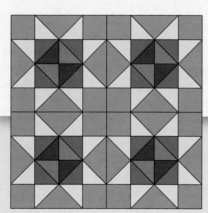

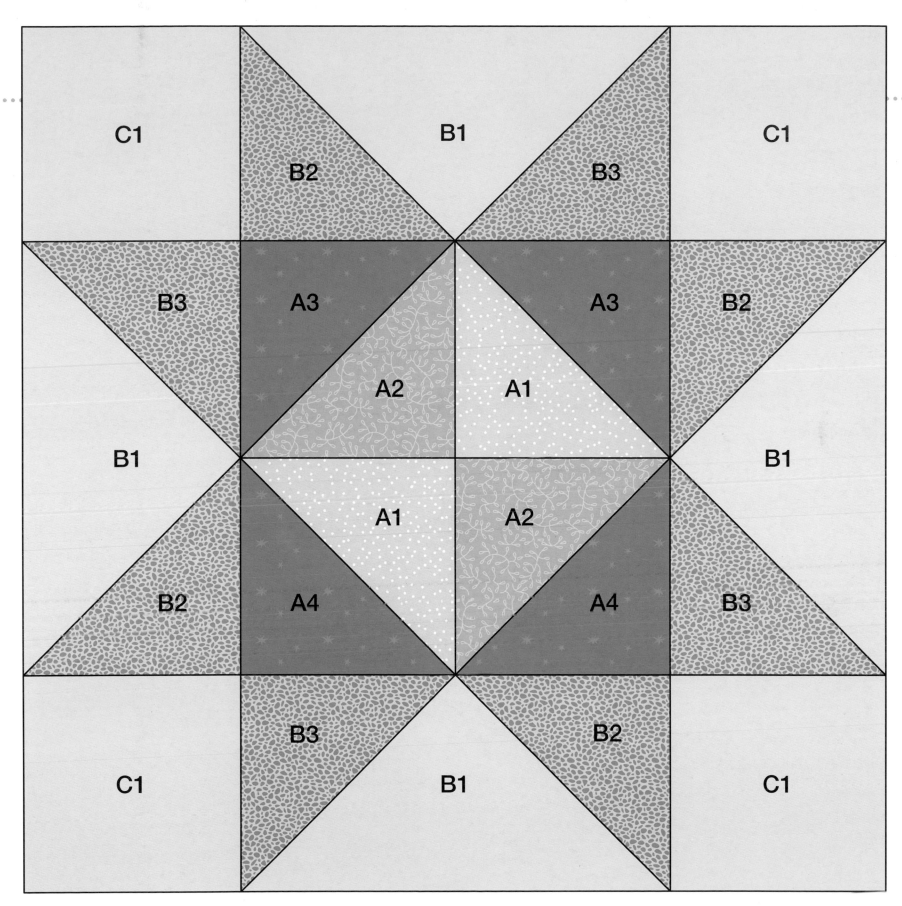

AUTUMN STAR *full-size block*

eight-pointed star

HOW TO CONSTRUCT THIS BLOCK

Sew A to Ar (4 times). Sew one short edge of C to A, stopping the stitching at seam line. Reposition edges and sew adjacent edge of C to Ar, starting stitching at seam line (4 times). Stitch two AArC units together, then stitch the remaining two AArC units together. Stitch these two units together to form a star. Stitch one edge of B to A edge, stopping stitching at seam line. Reposition edges and continue stitching adjacent edge of B to Ar edge, starting stitching at seam line. Repeat, stitching each B piece to AAr edges, being careful not to stitch through AAr seam lines. Sew a D strip to two opposite edges of star unit. Sew E to remaining two edges. Sew G to F (2 times). Sew Gr to F (2 times). Sew H to remaining G and Gr pieces (4 times). Sew HG and HGr units to GF and GrF units (4 times). Sew two GFH units to two opposite edges of star unit. Stitch two GGrFH units to remaining two edges of star unit to complete the block.

HOW TO MAKE THIS QUILT

This quilt is designed to be a full-size quilt measuring 78×87 inches. It uses a 3-inch-wide Checkerboard border. See page 213.

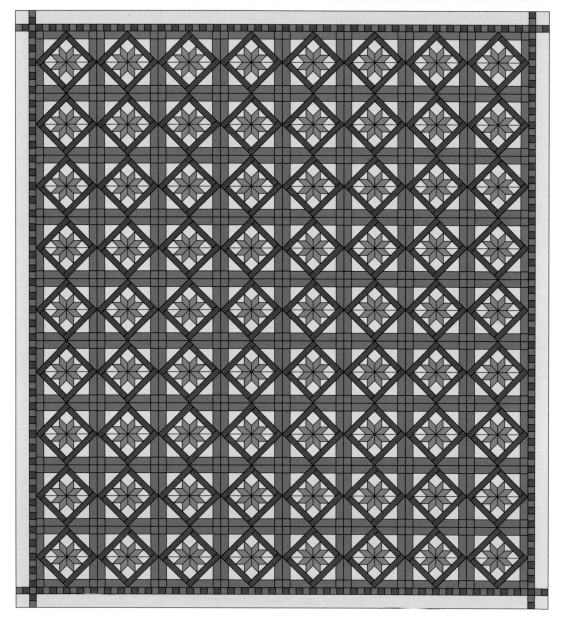

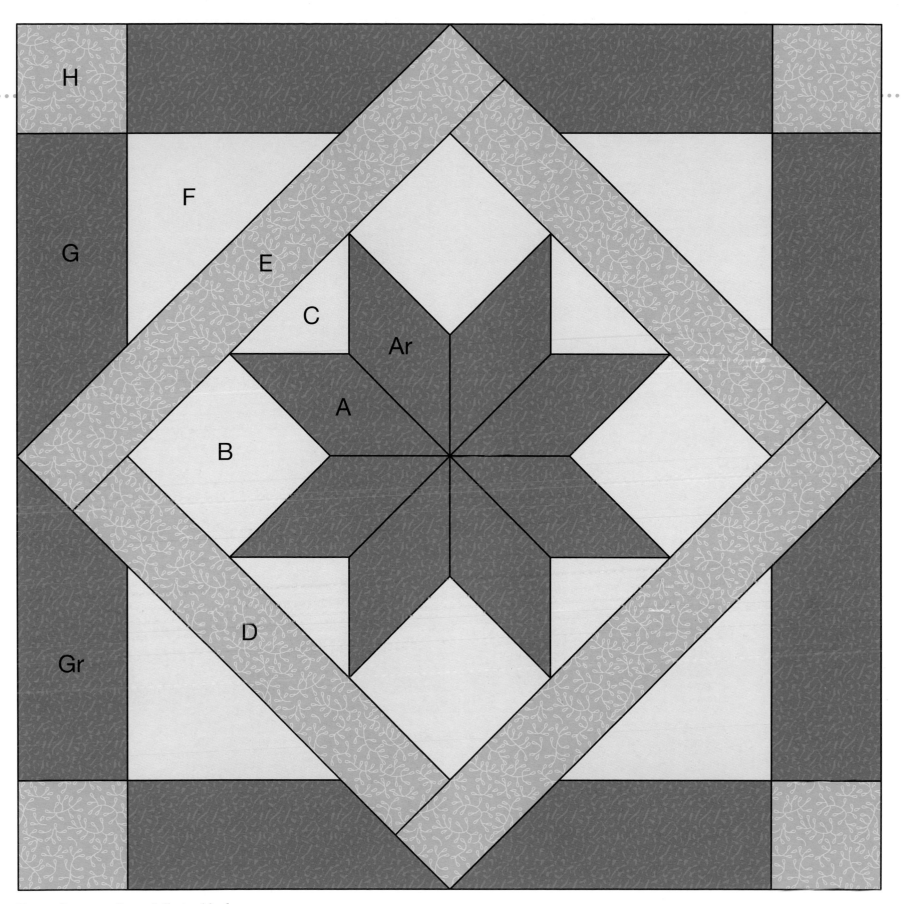

EIGHT-POINTED STAR *full-size block*

rotating star

HOW TO CONSTRUCT THIS BLOCK

Make 4 A sections by joining pieces in numerical order.
Make 4 B sections. Join a B section to each A section.
Join the 4 A B units to complete the block.

about this block

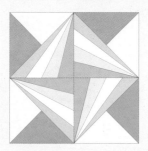

When making complicated stars or other patterns that are particularly intricate, try paper piecing. The prepared patchwork pieces are stitched together leaving the paper with the fabric. The paper is usually removed when the piecing is complete, but some early quilters, unable to afford batting, left papers on to add extra warmth. This technique is often used for piecing hexagons and diamonds.

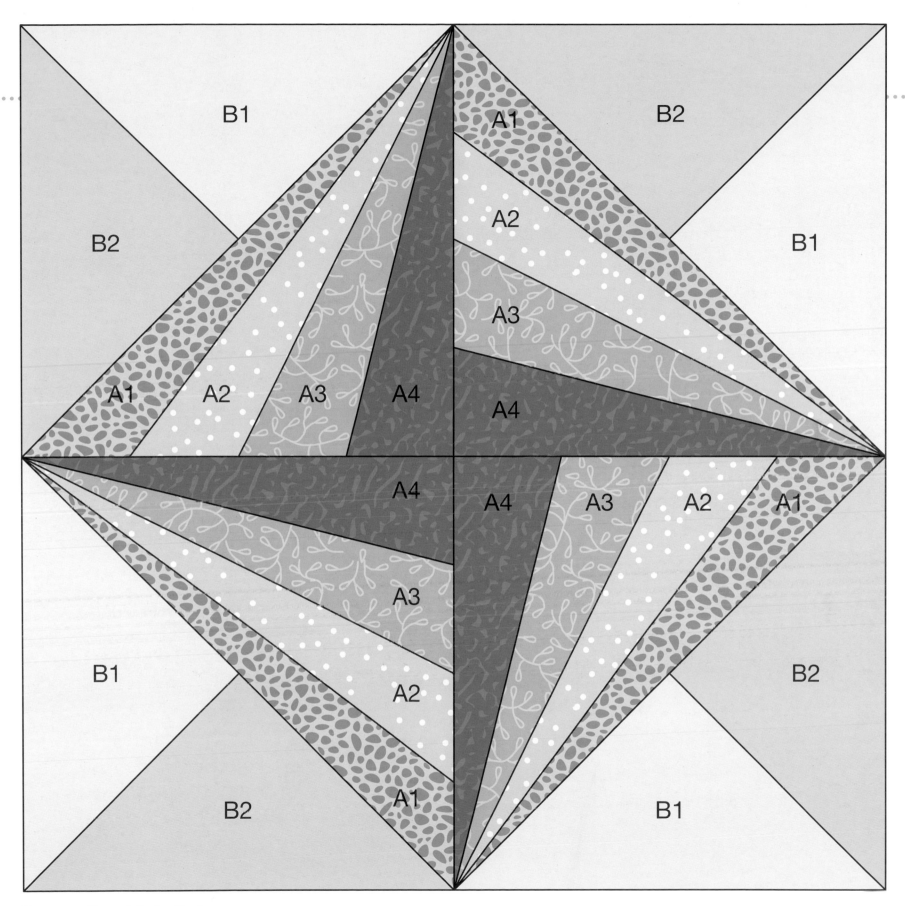

Rotating Star *full-size block*

stars and hearts

HOW TO CONSTRUCT THIS BLOCK

Sew B to A (4 times). Sew B to adjacent edge of each AB unit. Sew one BAB unit to one side of C then sew second BAB unit to opposite side of C to form center section. Sew D to one end of each of the remaining two BAB units. Sew second D to opposite ends of BAB units for side sections. Sew one side section to center section, then sew second side section to opposite side of center section. Sew E to one side of block, then sew E to opposite side. Sew F pieces to top and bottom edges of block. Applique G (heart pieces) onto A pieces, overlapping onto E and F pieces.

For an alternate fusing method of applique, see page 214.

HOW TO MAKE THIS QUILT

This quilt is designed to be a twin-size quilt measuring 70×95 inches. The blocks are turned on point and alternate with plain setting squares. It uses a 3-inch-wide solid-color border as shown with corner squares appliquéd with a single heart.

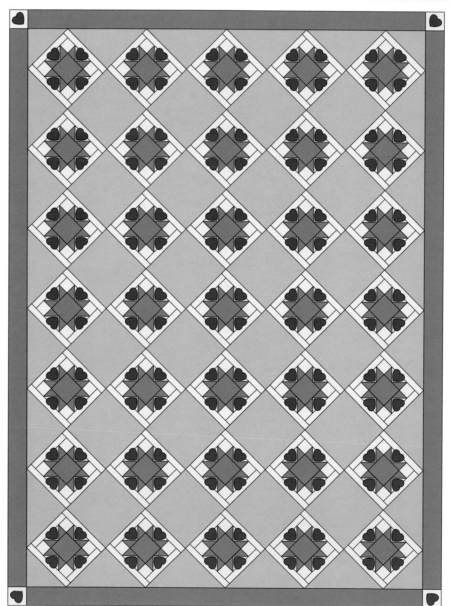

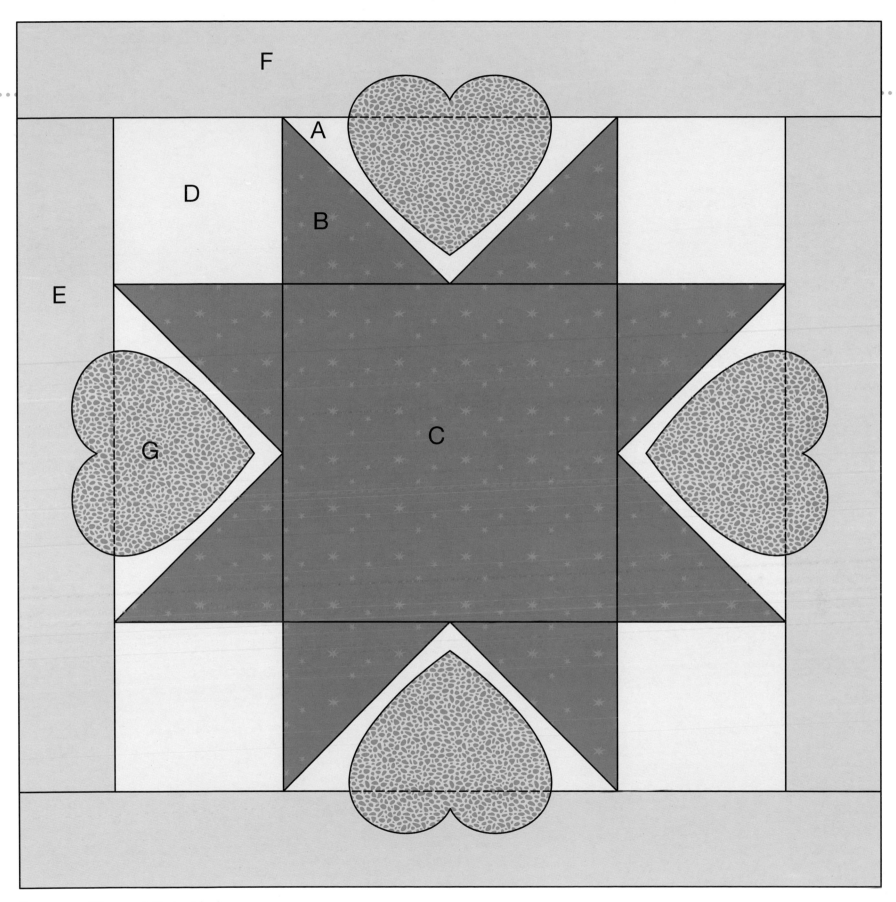

STARS AND HEARTS *full-size block*

heart patches

HOW TO CONSTRUCT THIS BLOCK

Sew B to each side of A. Sew B to top and bottom of A. Sew C to top and bottom of AB. Sew C to each side of AB. Sew D to D (8 times). Sew two DD units together (4 times). Sew another D to the D strip so that each of four strips has five D pieces sewn together. Sew a D strip to each side of previously completed block, sewing strips to two opposite sides first, then to remaining two sides. Sew E to each corner of block.

HOW TO MAKE THIS QUILT

This quilt is designed to be a twin-size quilt measuring 72×81 inches. It uses a 4½-inch-wide Triangles border. See page 208.

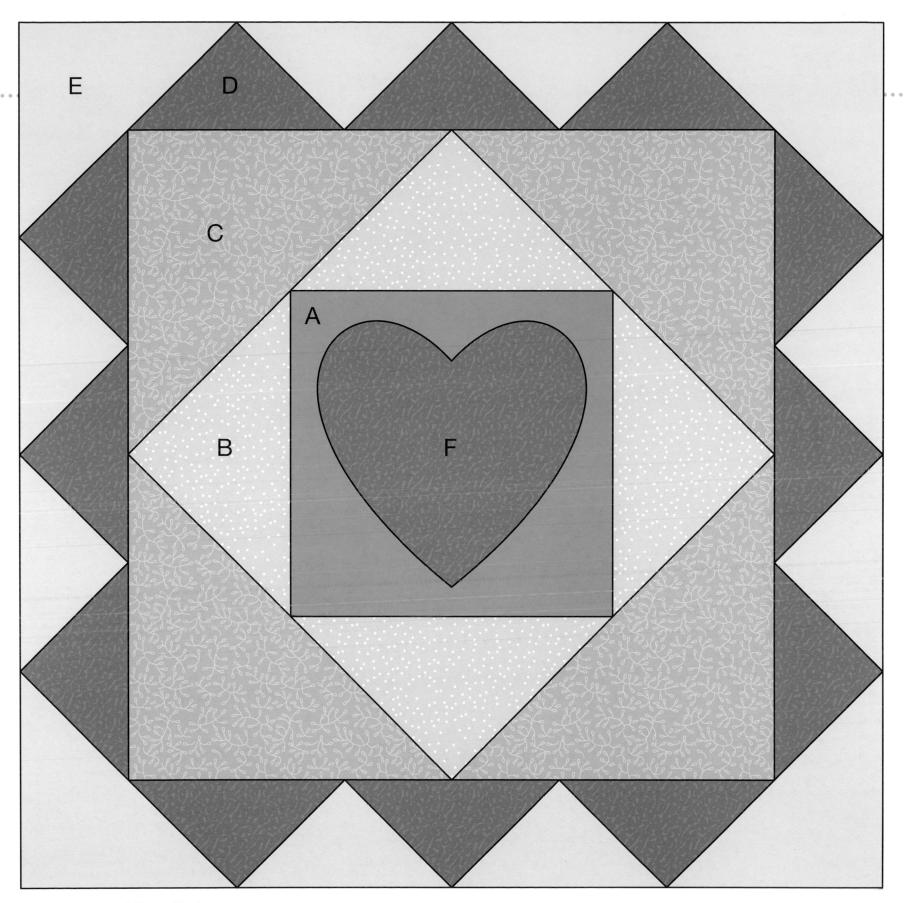

HEART PATCHES *full-size block*

rainbow stars

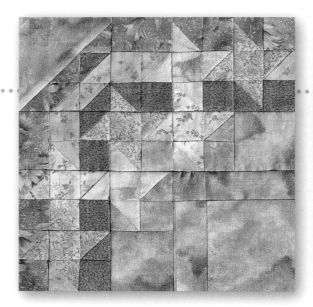

HOW TO CONSTRUCT THIS BLOCK

In chosen colors, lay out pieces in correct position. Be careful of placement. Sew A to A to make a half-square triangle (25 times). Row 1: Sew A to C; add AA. Sew B to ACAA. Sew ACAAB to AA; add B. Row 2: Sew A to AA; add B. Sew AAAB to AA; add B and AA. Sew AAABAABAA to B; add AA. Row 3: Sew A to (3)AA; add B. Sew A(3)AAB to AA; add B, AA, and another B. Sew Row 1 to Row 2. Add Row 3 to make Unit 1. Sew G to left side of Unit 1. Row 4: Sew B to AA; add B. Sew BAAB to AA; add B and another AA. Row 5: Sew AA to B; add AA. Sew AABAA to B; add AA and B. Sew Row 4 to Row 5 to make Unit 2. Sew C to left side of Unit 2. Sew E to right side of Unit 2. Row 6: Sew AA to B; add AA. Sew AABAA to B; add AA, B, and D to make Unit 3. Row 7: Sew B to AA; add B. Sew BAAB to AA; add B. Row 8: Sew AA to B; add AA. Row 9: Sew B to AA; add B. Sew Row 8 to Row 9. Add E. Sew Row 7 to Row 8 and 9. Add D and F to make Unit 4. Sew Units 1, 2, 3, and 4 together.

HOW TO MAKE THIS QUILT

This quilt is designed to be a twin-size quilt measuring 78×96 inches. It uses two 1½-inch-wide solid-colored borders as shown.

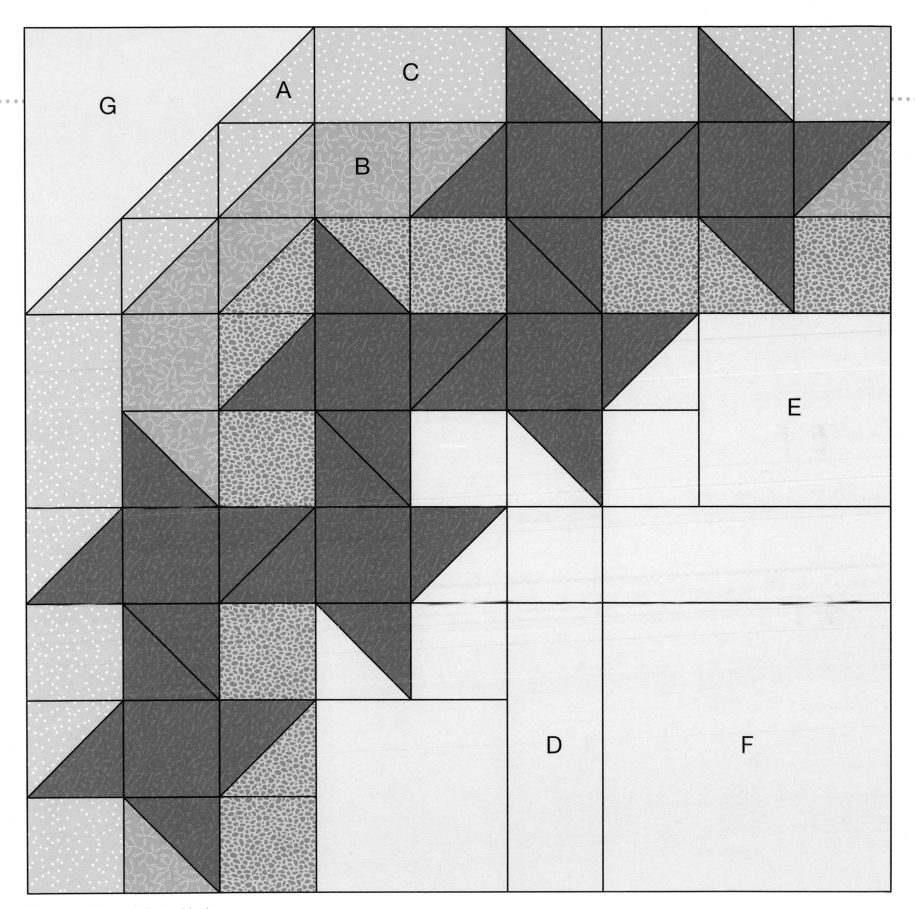

RAINBOW STARS *full-size block*

feathered star

HOW TO CONSTRUCT THIS BLOCK

Sew a light A to a dark A (24 times). Sew AA to AA (8 times); add AA (8 times). Lay out a left and right diagonal row of the three AAA triangle squares (4 times), placing the light side of the squares in the correct position. Left Side Diagonal Row: Sew a dark A triangle to the top of AAA (4 times). Sew B to the left side of AAAA (4 times). Sew short side of C to the right side of AAAAB (4 times). Right Side Diagonal Row: Sew a dark A triangle to the top of AAA (4 times). Sew a short side of a light triangle A to the bottom of AAAA (4 times). Sew B to the right side of AAAAA (4 times). Stitch the right side to the left side to make an ABC unit. Sew D to each side of ABC unit (2 times) to make Row 1 and Row 3. Sew ABC to E; add ABC to make Row 2. Stitch Row 1 to Row 2. Add Row 3 to complete the block.

HOW TO MAKE THIS QUILT

This quilt is designed to be a full- or queen-size quilt measuring 93×93 inches, including 2½-inch-wide sashing strips with setting squares. The inner border is 5 inches wide and the outer 2½-inch-wide border is made from combining the star points on the quilt block (an ABC unit).

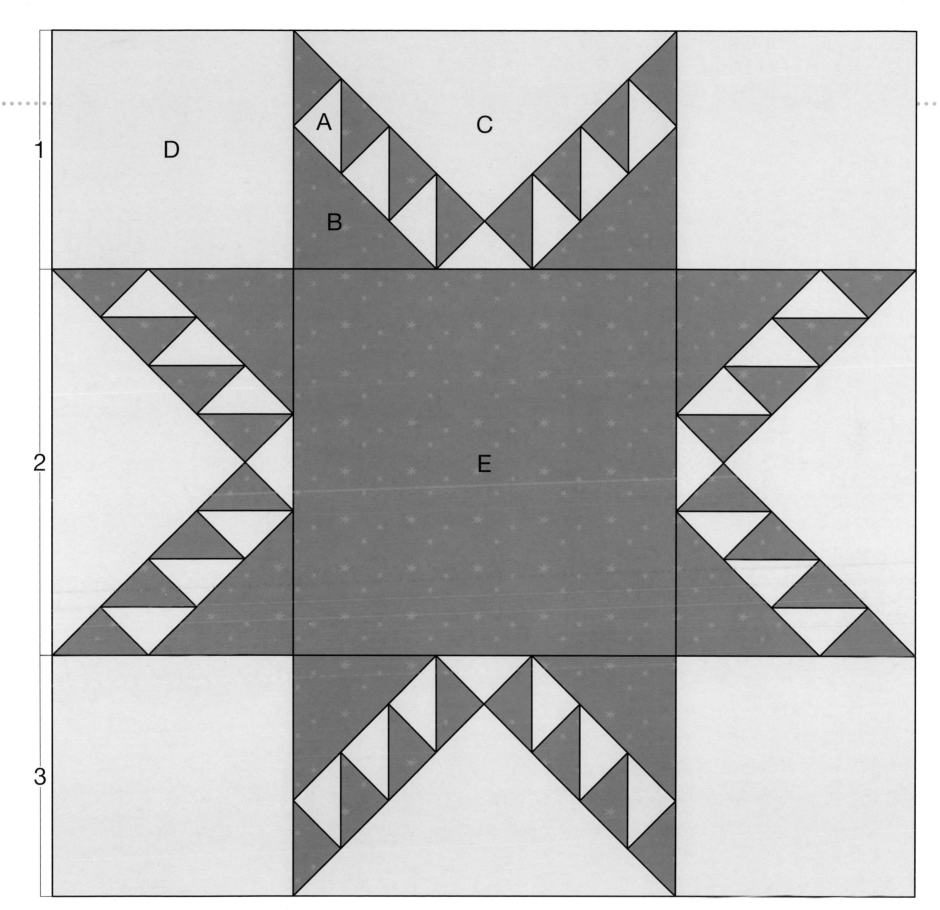

FEATHERED STAR *full-size block*

star shades

HOW TO CONSTRUCT THIS BLOCK

Sew A to B (4 times). Sew Ar to Br (4 times). Sew C to AB (4 times). Sew Cr to ArBr (4 times). Sew ABC to ArBrCr (4 times) to make four units. Stitch two units together (2 times). Join the units to complete the block.

HOW TO MAKE THIS QUILT

This quilt is designed to be a queen-size quilt measuring 90×99 inches. It includes 4½-inch-wide sashing strips with setting squares. The border is a 4½-inch-wide solid-color border with corner squares.

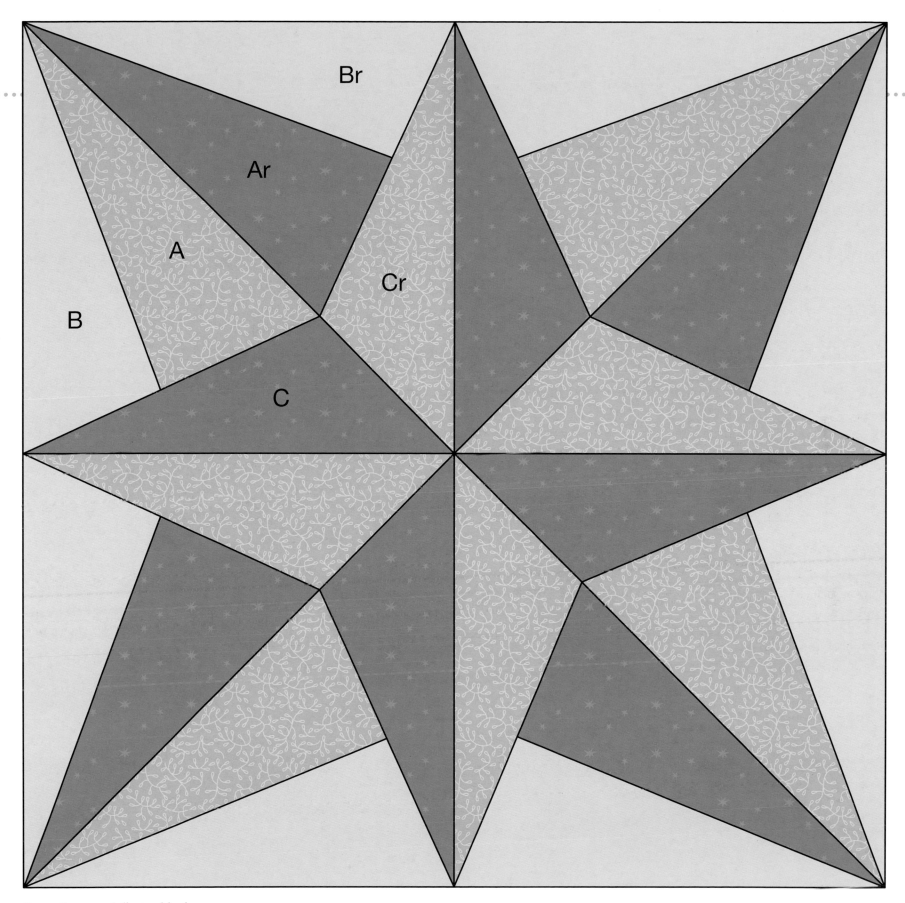

STAR SHADES *full-size block*

fireworks

HOW TO CONSTRUCT THIS BLOCK

Star unit: Sew B to A (4 times); add B (4 times). Sew C to BAB (2 times); add C (2 times). Sew BAB to D; add BAB. Sew CBABC to opposite sides of BABDBAB. Repeat (4 times). Stripe unit: Sew three Es together (4 times). Sew a star unit to opposite sides of a stripe unit (2 times) for Rows 1 and 3. Sew a stripe unit to opposite sides of a star unit for Row 2. Sew Rows 1, 2, and 3 together.

HOW TO MAKE THIS QUILT

This quilt is designed to be a twin-size quilt measuring 68×86 inches. We have used a 3-inch-wide plain border and four 1-inch-wide solid-color borders. One corner star from the nine-patch block is used in the corners of the borders. We suggest quilting stars in the plain setting squares we've placed between the pieced blocks.

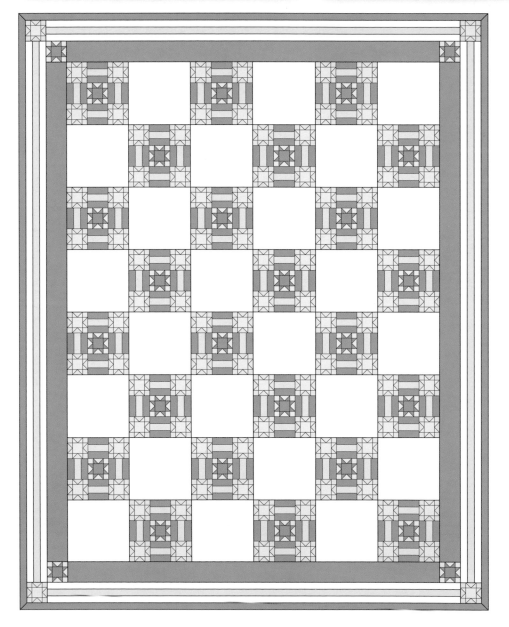

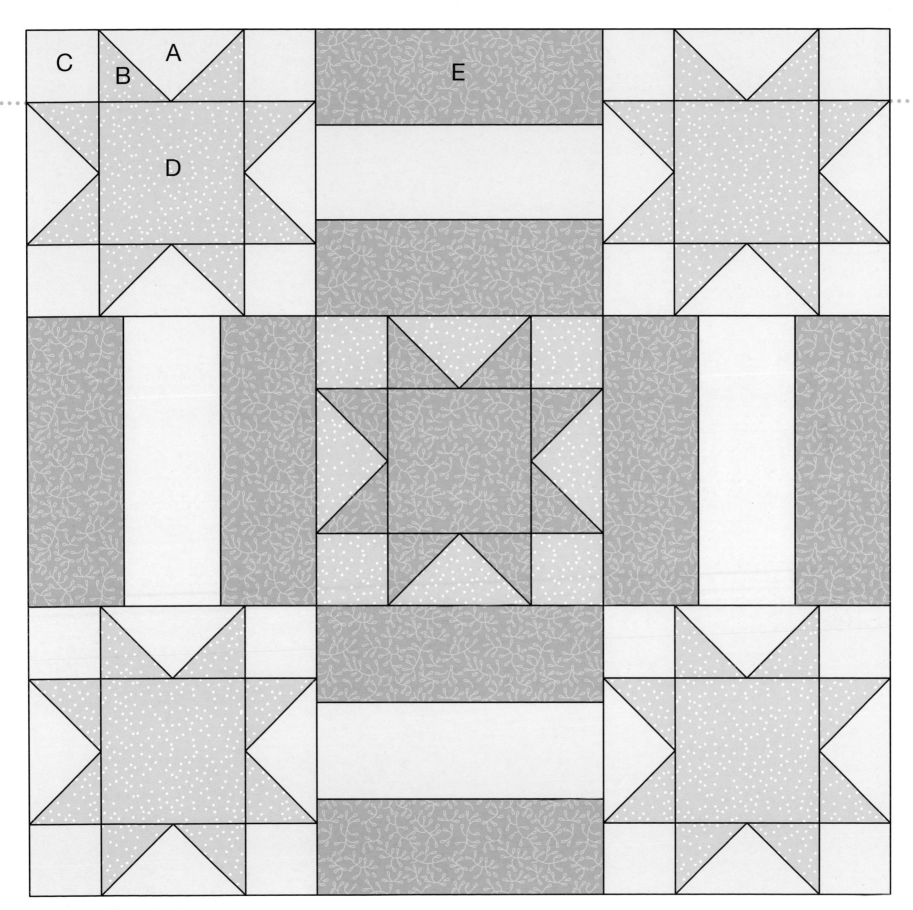

FIREWORKS *full-size block*

tile heart

HOW TO CONSTRUCT THIS BLOCK

Mark a ¼-inch seam allowance around the outside edge of a 9½-inch background square, using a quilter's pencil or water-soluble pen.

Spacing is critical to the look of this block, and basting the seam allowance under on each piece is recommended. After appliqué pieces have been basted, arrange pieces, beginning with A, on the background square. Each appliqué piece is separated by a ¼-inch space, allowing the background to frame the appliquéd pieces. Carefully measure the ¼-inch seam allowance space. Pin or baste in place and appliqué pieces with matching threads. Remove the ¼-inch markings on the quilt block.

HOW TO MAKE THIS QUILT

This quilt is designed to be a twin-size quilt measuring 72×90 inches, including 4½-inch-wide sashing and a 9-inch-wide border.

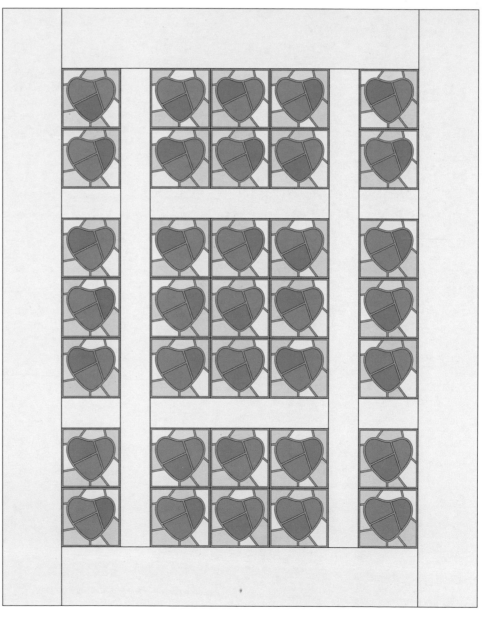

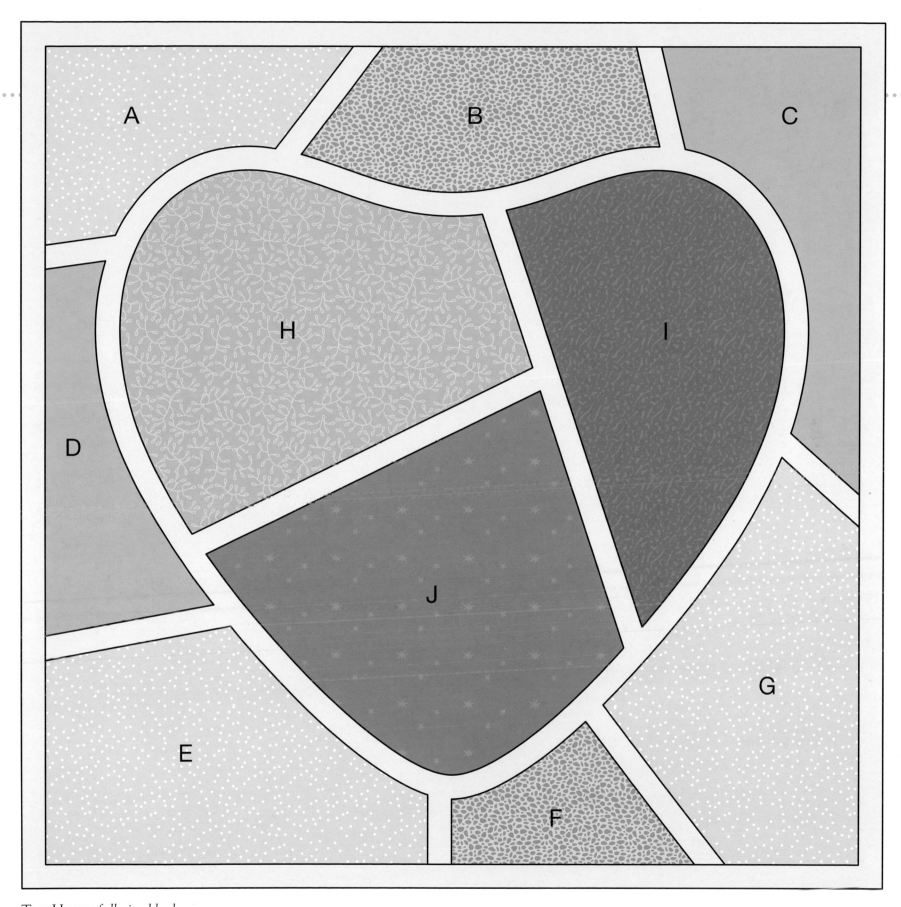

Tɪʟᴇ Hᴇᴀʀᴛ *full-size block*

Florals, in all of their beauty, bring loveliness to everything they touch. The glorious colors, interesting shapes, and intriguing textures of these natural works of art are an inspiration for quilters everywhere.

INSPIRATION

The love of florals and images of flowers have been a common theme for quilters for centuries. One of the earliest forms of quiltmaking, the Borderie Perse, was popular in the 1700s when chintz was the fabric of choice. These glazed fabrics were block printed and featured designs of flowers, figures, and nature. Shipped in from England and France, these cherished fabrics were expensive and every image on the fabric was used.

Paper albums inscribed with verses and autographs became popular in the 1820s, a fad encouraged by the new influential magazine, *Godey's Lady's Book*. By 1840 the album craze extended to quilts.

Between 1840 and 1860 an important trend was the creative, elaborate floral appliqué that started in Pennsylvania and Maryland and then spread to other areas.

The Baltimore Album quilts were mostly appliqué, and the women apparently strove to outdo one another with elaborate creations of bouquets, wreaths, and cornucopias.

Wreaths were a favorite theme of the women who made these quilts. There were wreaths of fruit, laurel leaves, tulips, and the most beloved—roses and buds.

Florals continued to be favorites as women began to piece as well as appliqué quilts. Favorite floral patterns such as Carolina Lily, Dogwood, Laurel Wreath, Flower Pots, Swirling Peony, Star Flower, Springtime Blossoms, and Spiced Pinks were the beginning of the natural love affair between florals and quilts.

During the Great Depression, quilts were based on traditional patterns and techniques, but often had soft colors and floral themes such as the classic Grandma's Flower Garden. These soft, sometimes elegant, designs contrasted with the stark reality of the hard times facing quiltmakers. By concentrating on making something beautiful, the quilter could block out poverty and deprivation.

Quiltmakers during the 1920s and 1930s clamored for new ideas and patterns and publishers responded with quilting patterns

ABOVE *Floral designs have always graced many useful items found in kitchens and homes. This mixing bowl made by the Jewel Tea company in about 1930 features florals around the top edge of the bowl.*

that could be ordered by mail. Many of the patterns featured floral designs that are still treasured today.

LEFT *Architectual pieces also reflect the love of florals. This ceramic tile piece with its geometric floral design is dated 1891 and was the decorative element around a fireplace.*
RIGHT *These beautiful English tea mugs manufactured in this century have floral designs inside and out.*

floral appliqué

HOW TO CONSTRUCT THIS BLOCK

Fold a 10-inch background square in quarters, lightly press. Arrange each piece on the square beginning with A. Appliqué all pieces in place with matching threads. Trim block to 9½ inches square.

HOW TO MAKE THIS QUILT

This quilt is designed to be a queen-size quilt measuring 99×108 inches with a top designed to wrap over head pillows. Four central blocks are outlined with a 2¼-inch-wide pink mitered border, then a 4½-inch-wide blue mitered inner border. The pink border is 4½ inches wide, the blue side and bottom outer borders are 9 inches wide, and the blue top border is 18 inches.

FLORAL APPLIQUÉ *full-size block*

embroidered basket

HOW TO CONSTRUCT THIS BLOCK

Sew A to B; add C. To ABC, add D. Sew G and Gr to ABCD. Sew E to F. Set in EF to ABCDGGr, stopping the stitching at the seam line. Reposition EF and begin stitching at the seam line, stopping the stitching at the next seam line. Reposition EF and begin stitching at the seam line. Appliqué I to H. Stitch IH to basket unit. Using the stitch diagrams on page 214, work stem stitches to embroider the flowers. Fill in the small berrylike flowers with satin stitches.

HOW TO MAKE THIS QUILT

This quilt is designed to be a full-size quilt measuring 79½×92¼ inches, including 4⅞-inch-wide inner border strips to frame the top and bottom of the basket block section and 7½-inch-wide inner border strips at the sides. Setting triangles alternate with outer basket border blocks.

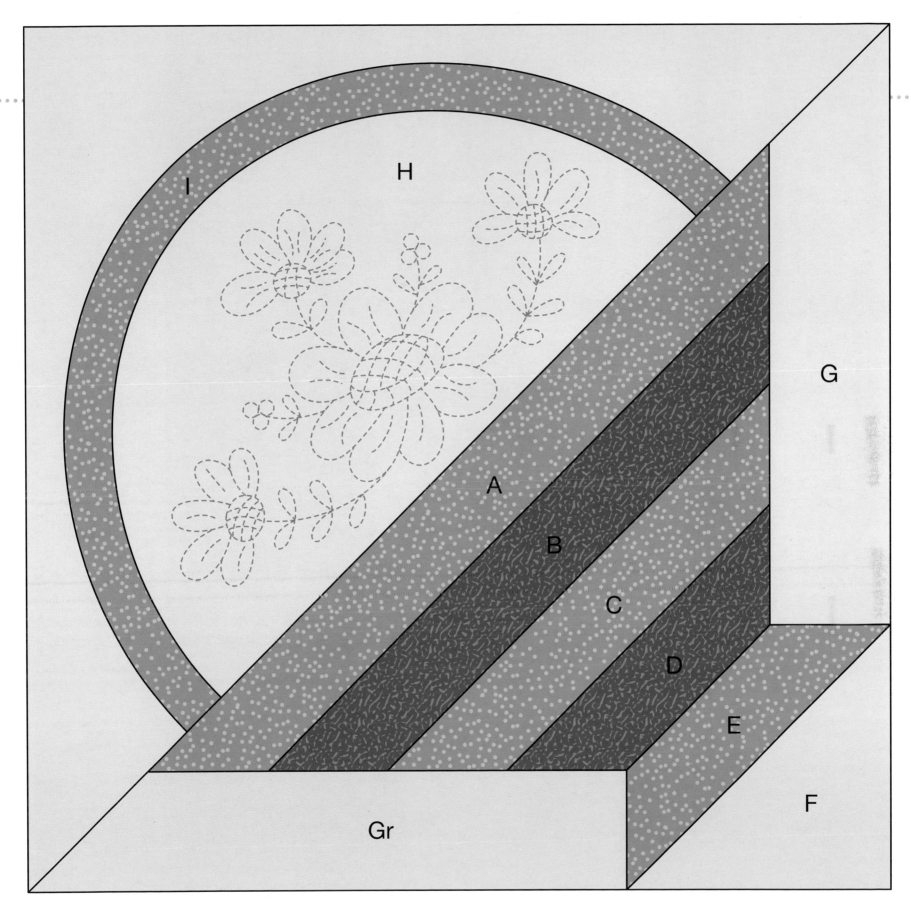

I

H

G

A

B

C

D

E

F

Gr

Embroidered Basket *full-size block*

texas tulip

HOW TO CONSTRUCT THIS BLOCK

Appliqué F to E, using matching thread. Sew G and Gr to two adjacent sides of EF. Sew H and Hr to remaining two adjacent sides of EFGGr. Stitch B to A (4 times). Fold AB background square diagonally once; press. Arrange each piece, beginning with C, onto the background square. Appliqué all pieces in place with matching threads.

HOW TO MAKE THIS QUILT

This quilt is designed to be a full-size quilt measuring 81×99 inches, including 4½-inch-wide borders.

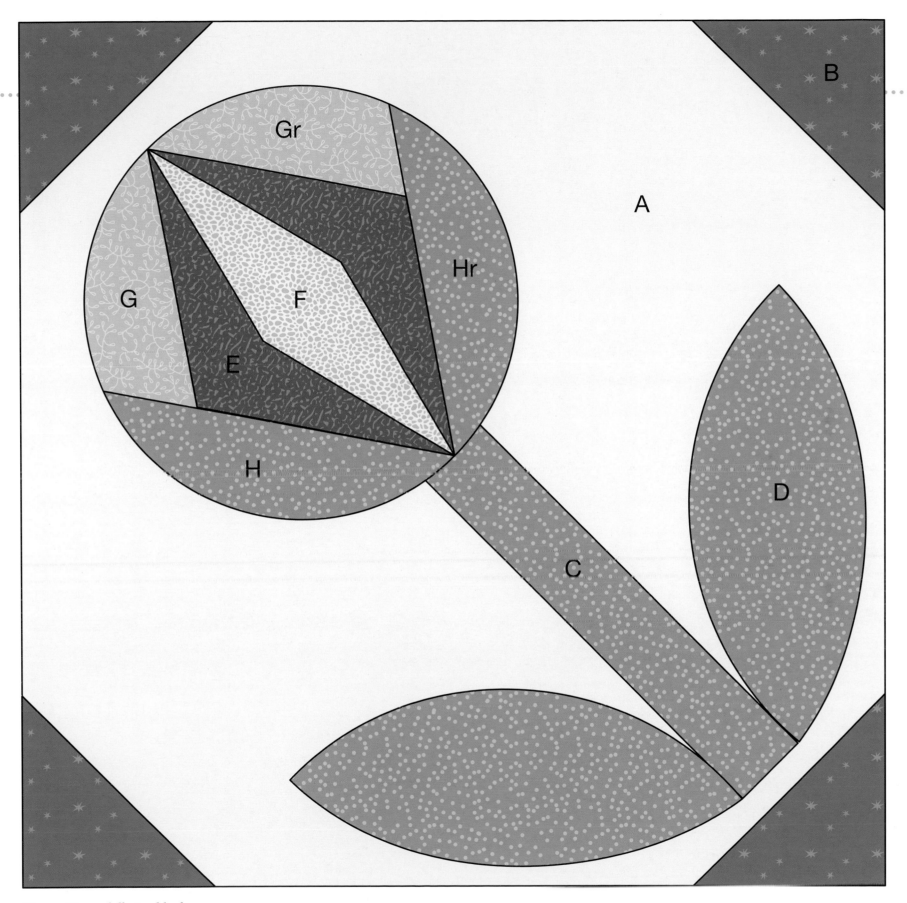

T EXAS T ULIP *full-size block*

floral sunburst

HOW TO CONSTRUCT THIS BLOCK

Fold a 10-inch background square in quarters; press. Fold diagonally in both directions; lightly press. Arrange each piece, beginning with A. Appliqué all pieces in place with matching threads. Trim block to 9½ inches square.

HOW TO MAKE THIS QUILT

This quilt is designed to be a queen-size quilt measuring 90×103½ inches. It uses 4½-inch-wide sashing strips created from two 1⅛-inch-wide strips and one 2¼-inch-wide strip and setting squares made from the Fireworks block on page 52. The border is a 9-inch-wide solid-color border with larger Fireworks blocks in the corners.

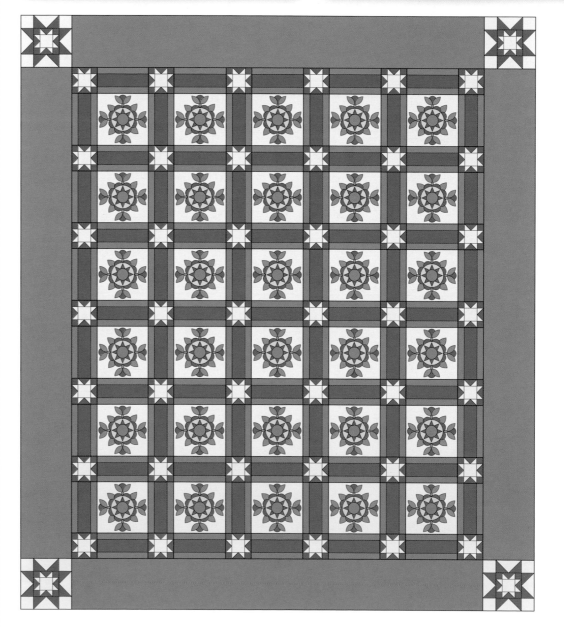

Floral Sunburst *full-size block*

pansies

HOW TO CONSTRUCT THIS BLOCK

Appliqué leaf and flower pieces for each pansy in place on the background fabric.

about this block

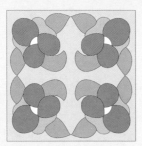

Appliquéd flowers of all kinds can be created by fusing the parts of the flower to the main block and then using machine appliqué to stitch around each piece. To create your own pattern for your favorite flower, look in seed catalogs or wallpaper pattern books for photos or designs that you might be able to translate into a beautiful appliquéd floral block.

Pansies *full-size block*

cornucopia

HOW TO CONSTRUCT THIS BLOCK

Fold a 10-inch background square diagonally twice in an X and press. Lay out the appliqué pieces and pin in place. Beginning with A, appliqué each piece in order alphabetically with matching threads. Trim the background square to measure 9½ inches. Using the diagrams on page 214, stem-stitch the leaf veins, cornucopia detail, and flower stems. The flower centers are satin-stitched with a stem-stitch outline.

HOW TO MAKE THIS QUILT

This quilt is designed to be a twin- or full-size quilt measuring 81×94½ inches, including a 4½-inch-wide mitered sashing and a 4½-inch-wide mitered border on three sides. To serve as a pillow covering, the header is 18×81 inches.

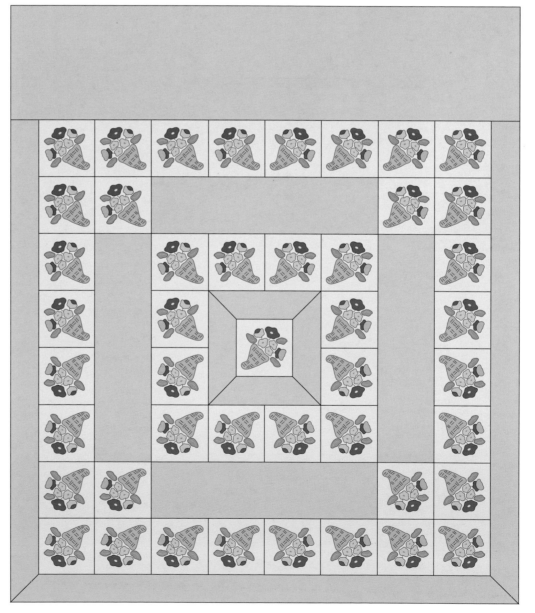

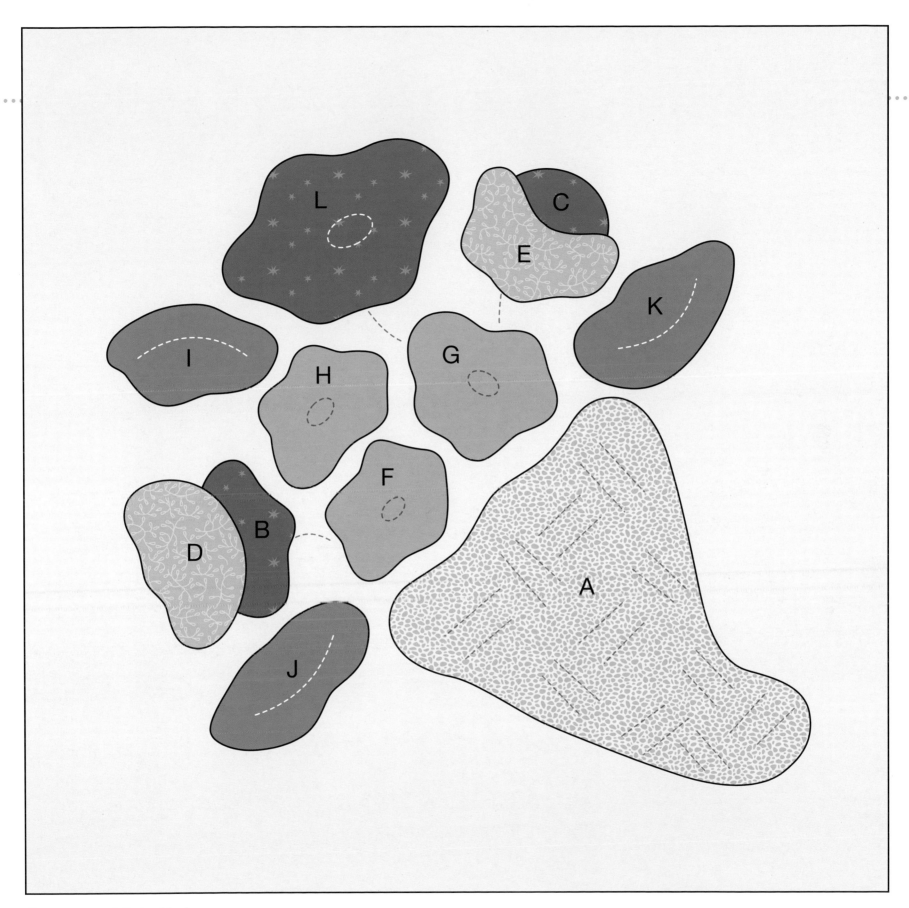

CORNUCOPIA *full-size block*

flower basket

HOW TO CONSTRUCT THIS BLOCK

Sew B to A. Sew C to BA. Sew D to CBA. Sew E to DCBA. Sew F to EDCBA. Sew G to FEDCBA. Sew H to I and H to Ir. Sew HI and HIr units to each side of basket. Sew J to basket to complete half of block. Appliqué handle to K. Join the two halves to form a square. Make yo-yos (see page 126), and sew to K, attaching pieces at circles marked M.

HOW TO MAKE THIS QUILT

This quilt is designed to be a queen-size quilt measuring 80×104½ inches. It uses 4½-inch-wide sashing strips and setting squares, a 4½-inch- wide light pink inner border, and two 2-inch-wide darker pink borders.

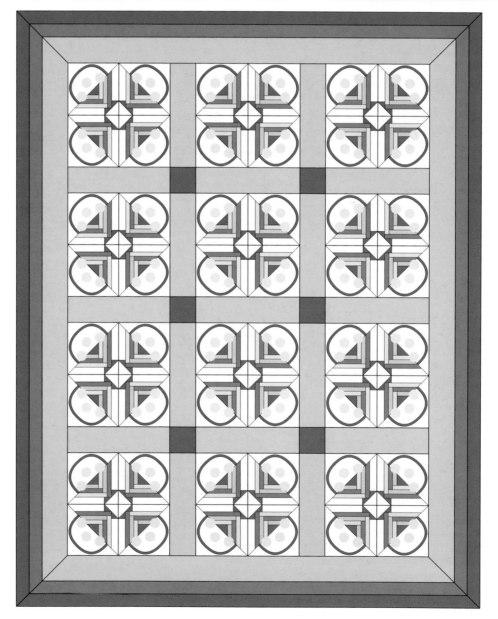

OHIO ROSE *full-size block*

peony

HOW TO CONSTRUCT THIS BLOCK

Sew medium A to background B; add medium Ar. Sew ABAr to D. Applique E onto ABAD with matching thread. Sew a dark Ar to A (2 times). Sew ArA to ArA. Sew AArAAr to ABArDE. Set in triangle B to AAr (3 times). Stop the stitching at the seam line. Reposition B and begin stitching at the seam line. Be careful not to stitch through the AAr seam. Set in C (2 times), stopping the stitching at the seam line as above.

HOW TO MAKE THIS QUILT

This quilt is designed to be a full-size quilt measuring 81×90 inches, including 9-inch-wide inner and outer borders with corner blocks. The corner blocks in the Peony block border use a variation of the block (using only pieces A, Ar, B, and C), creating a star motif.

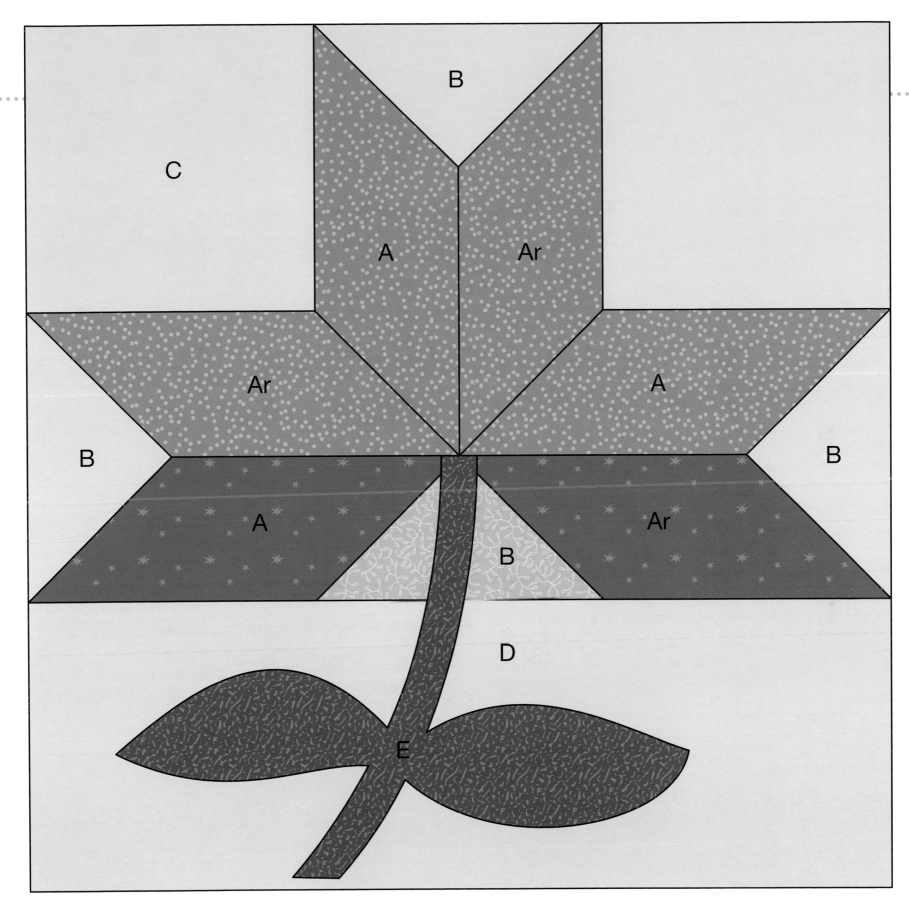

PEONY *full-size block*

martha's vineyard

HOW TO CONSTRUCT THIS BLOCK

Fold a 9½-inch background square diagonally twice; press. Cut twenty-two 1½-inch circles to make 22 yo-yos for grapes. Beginning with A, lay out each pattern piece and pin in place. Unpin part of C and appliqué A. Appliqué the B and Br leaves in place, using matching threads. Appliqué stem C in place. Using a stem stitch (see page 214), embroider vein lines on leaves following the pattern markings. Add the yo-yos (see page 126), following the placement lines to complete the block.

HOW TO MAKE THIS QUILT

This quilt is designed to be a full-size quilt measuring 90×90 inches, including 9-inch setting squares.

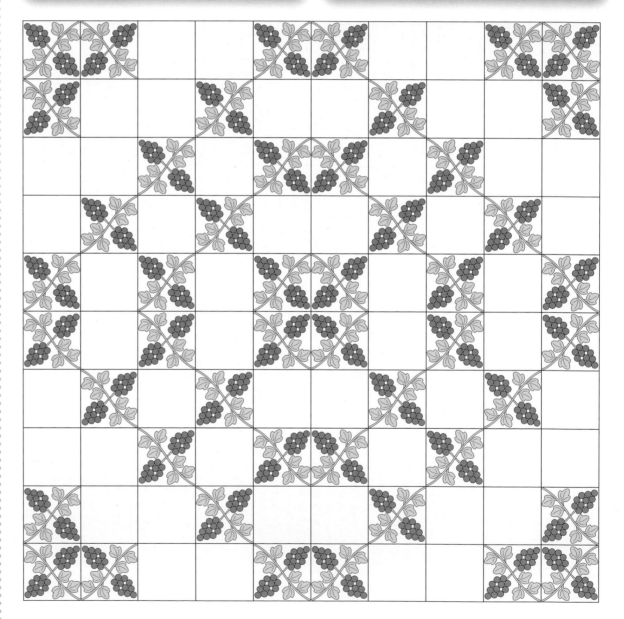

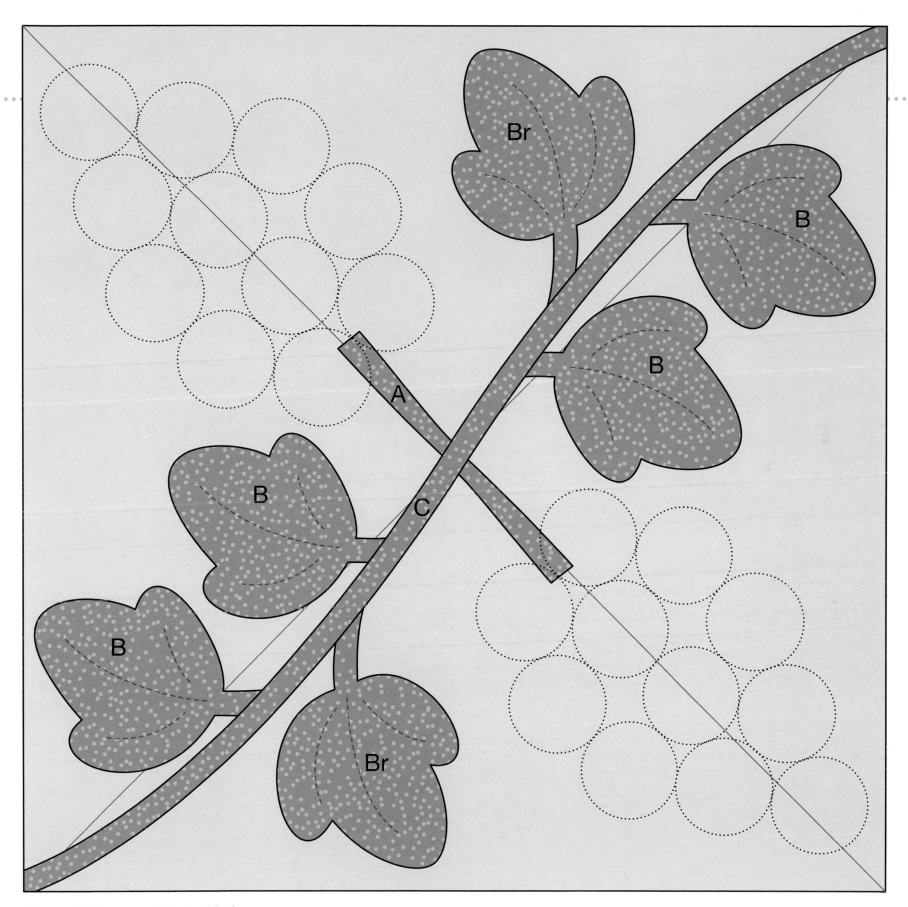

Martha's Vineyard *full-size block*

floral fancies

HOW TO CONSTRUCT THIS BLOCK

Arrange pieces A through Gr onto background piece. Appliqué C, E, and Er pieces. Appliqué the A pieces, slightly overlapping ends of the C piece. Appliqué the B pieces on top of the A pieces. Appliqué the F pieces, slightly overlapping ends of E piece. Appliqué the G and Gr pieces, slightly overlapping the E, Er, and F pieces. Appliqué the D pieces.

For an alternate fusing method of appliqué, see page 214.

HOW TO MAKE THIS QUILT

This quilt is designed to be a twin-size quilt measuring 67×89 inches. It uses 2-inch-wide sashing strips, a 1-inch-wide solid color border, and a 4-inch-wide solid color border.

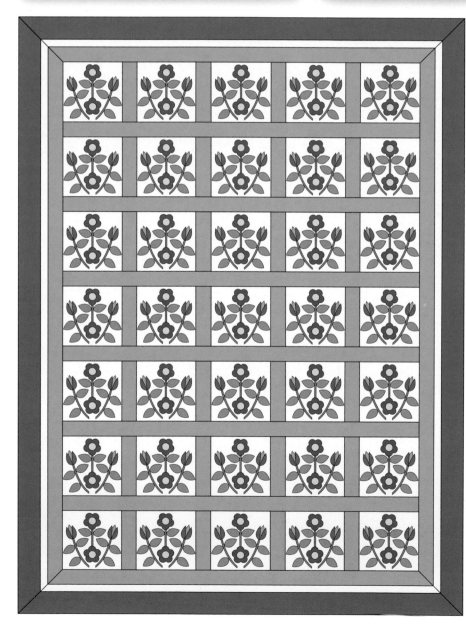

Floral Fancies *full-size block*

carolina lily

HOW TO CONSTRUCT THIS BLOCK

Unit 1: Sew A to A to make a square. Add A to each side of AA. Sew A to B (2 times). Sew AAAA to ABA. Add C. Unit 2: Sew A to A to make a square (4 times). Sew AA to AA (2 times). Add A (2 times). Stitch AAAAA to D (2 times). Add C (2 times). Unit 3: Sew E to each side of F. Stitch Unit 1 to Unit 2. Stitch Unit 2 to Unit 3. Sew Unit 1-2 to Unit 2-3.

HOW TO MAKE THIS QUILT

This quilt is designed to be a king-size quilt measuring 100½×120 inches, including 2⅜-inch-wide mitered sashing, a 4½-inch-wide mitered inner border, and the Triangles border. See page 208.

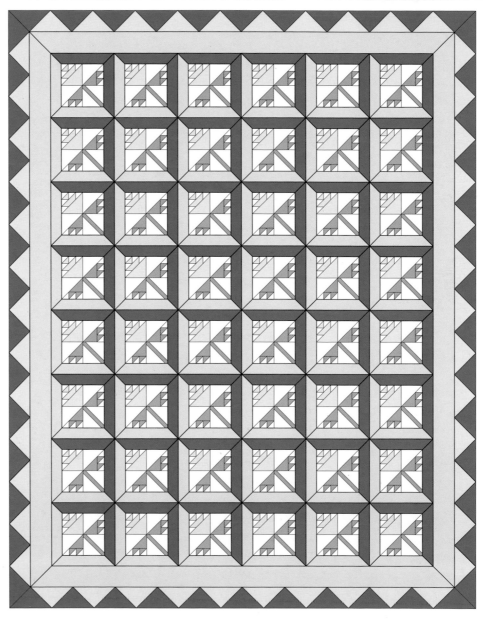

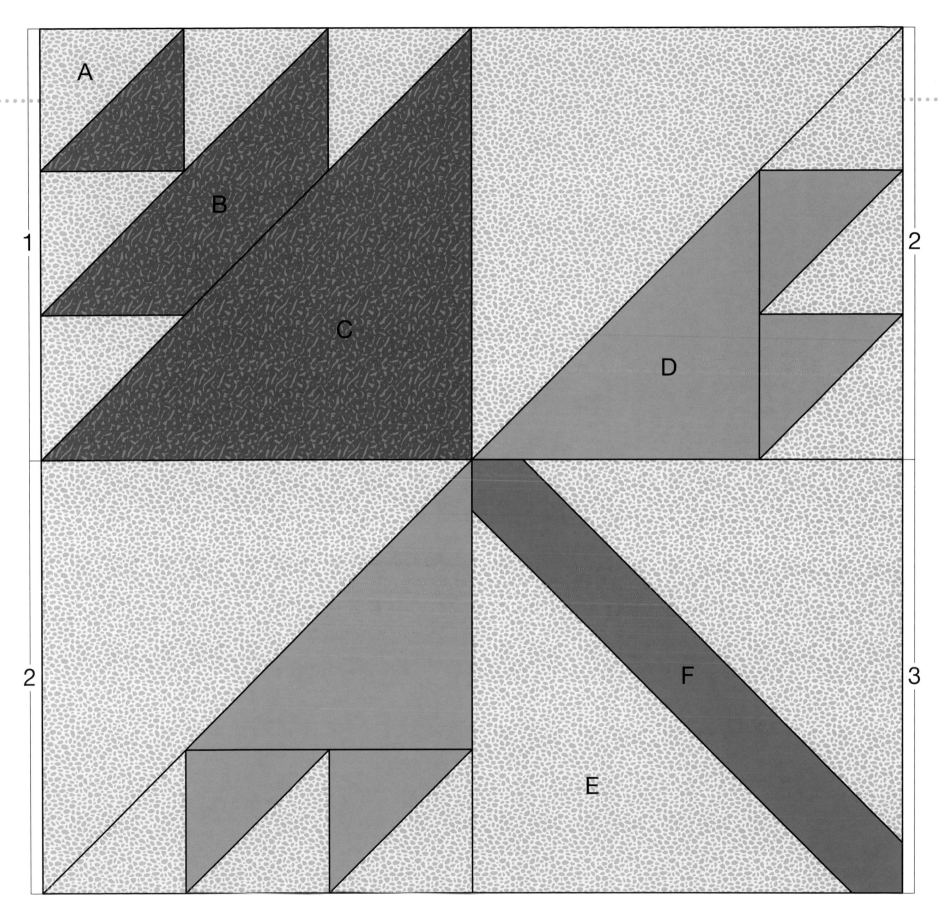

CAROLINA LILY *full-size block*

tulip

HOW TO CONSTRUCT THIS BLOCK

Sew B to two adjacent sides of A. Sew C to D and Cr to Dr. Then sew CD to E and CrDr to Er. Sew F to CDE unit and Fr to the CrDrEr unit. Then add in the following order; G and Gr pieces, and H pieces. Sew one side of the AB unit to the top edge of piece E. Stop stitching ¼" from the end of stitching line at the center point (where the top edges of E and Er join). Repeat on the other side, joining AB to Er. Sew the center seam, stitching from the top down along E, D, and G edges.

HOW TO MAKE THIS QUILT

This quilt is designed to be an extra-long twin-size quilt measuring 71×107 inches. It uses 2-inch sashing strips and a 4-inch-wide solid color border as shown.

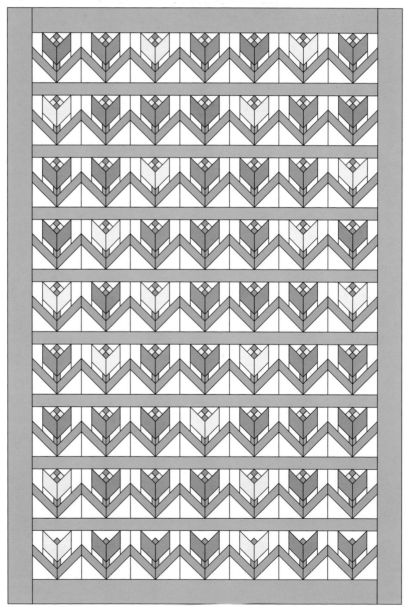

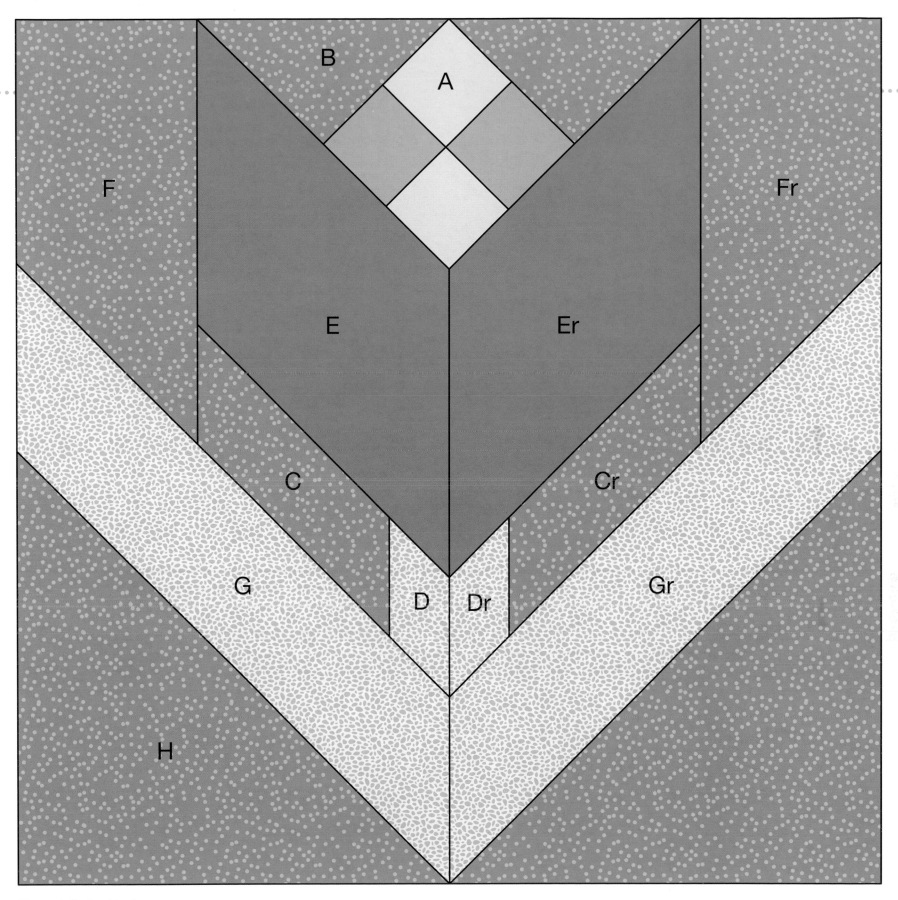

Tulip *full-size block*

poppies

HOW TO CONSTRUCT THIS BLOCK

Fold a 10-inch background square diagonally twice in an X and press. Beginning with A, lay out each piece and pin in place, using the pressed lines as a placement guide. Using matching threads, appliqué each piece in alphabetical order. Trim the block to measure 9½ inches square.

HOW TO MAKE THIS QUILT

This quilt is designed to be a queen-size quilt measuring 90×108 inches, including a 9-inch-wide pieced inner border with corner blocks. The center section uses 18-inch plain corner squares. The outer border is 9 inches wide with corner blocks.

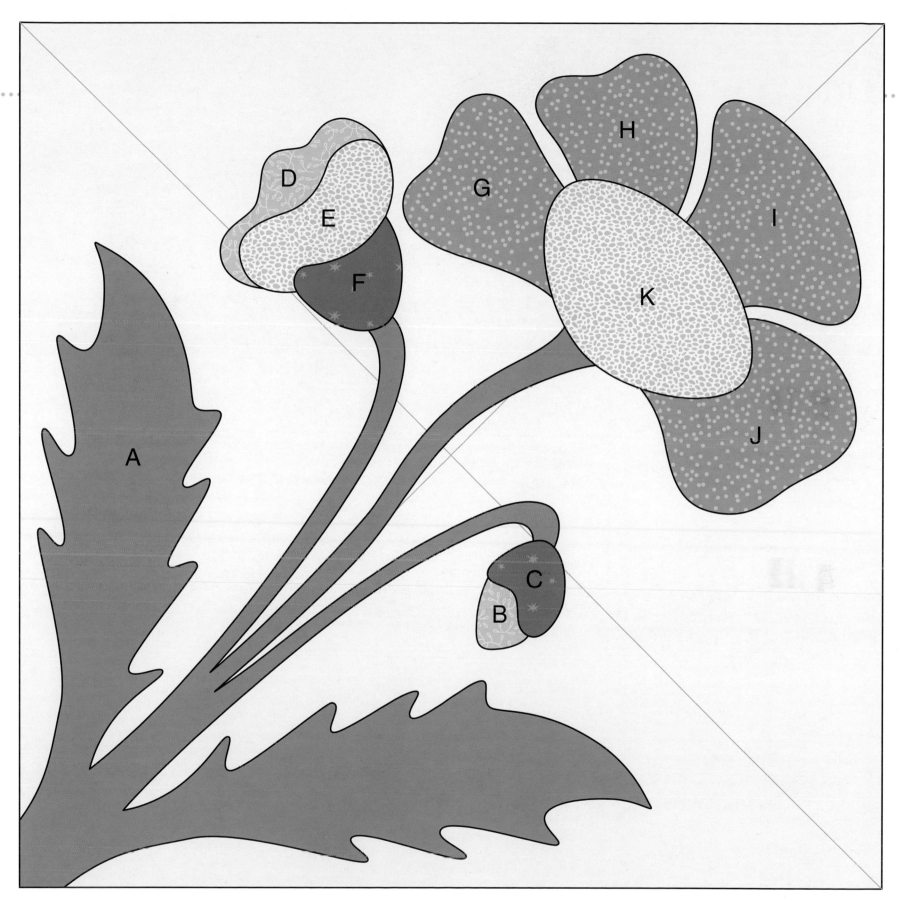

Poppies *full-size block*

spiced pinks

HOW TO CONSTRUCT THIS BLOCK

Sew A to B (4 times). Sew the 4 AB units together to form the square in the center of block. Appliqué D, E, G, and F pieces (stem, leaves, flowers) to each C piece (see page 214 to make appliqué blocks.) Add C to AB unit (4 times).

about this block

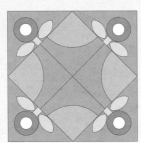

Combining piecing and appliqué can make for an interesting look and a lovely finished quilt. This block is both pieced and machine-appliqued. Using the machine-appliqué method on the round shapes with the pieced block keeps the block smoother and more even.

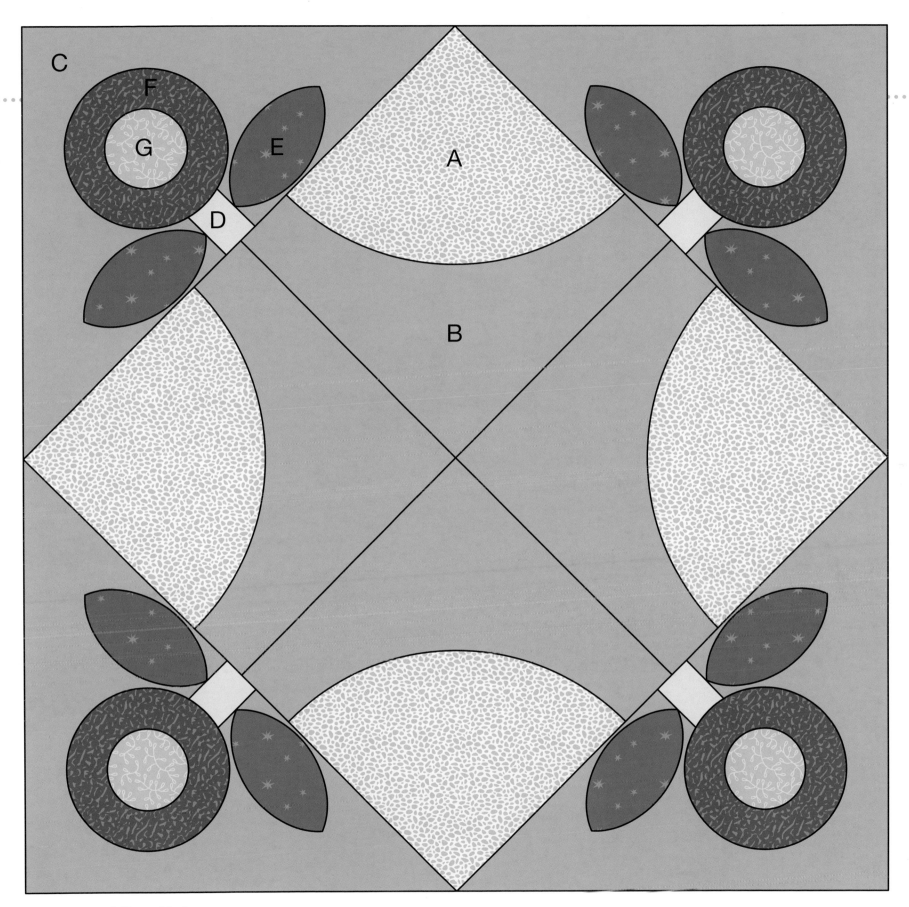

C

F

G

E

D

A

B

Spiced Pinks *full-size block*

prairie point flower

HOW TO CONSTRUCT THIS BLOCK

Cut four 1½-inch squares and fold into 4 prairie points (P pieces). (For prairie point instructions see page 215.) Sew P to A2 to make AP unit. (Note: A1 and A2 are the same size.) Make 4 A-P units. Join the units to complete the block, stitching the long edge of each prairie point into the seam of the A1 and A2 pieces to make a triangle. Sew a button to the center.

about this block

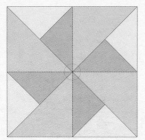

Add embellishments to a favorite block pattern to change the entire look of the finished block. Prairie points are squares of fabric that are folded into triangles to be used as edgings or to be sewn into the seams of the block. The folded fabric adds interest and dimension to the block.

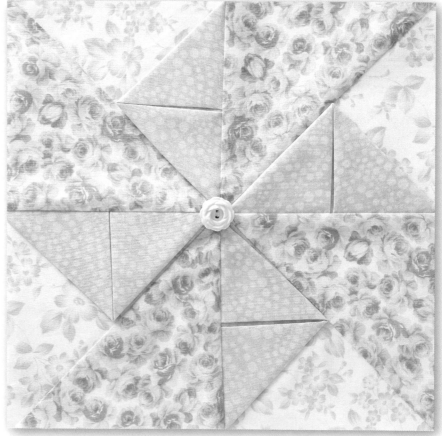

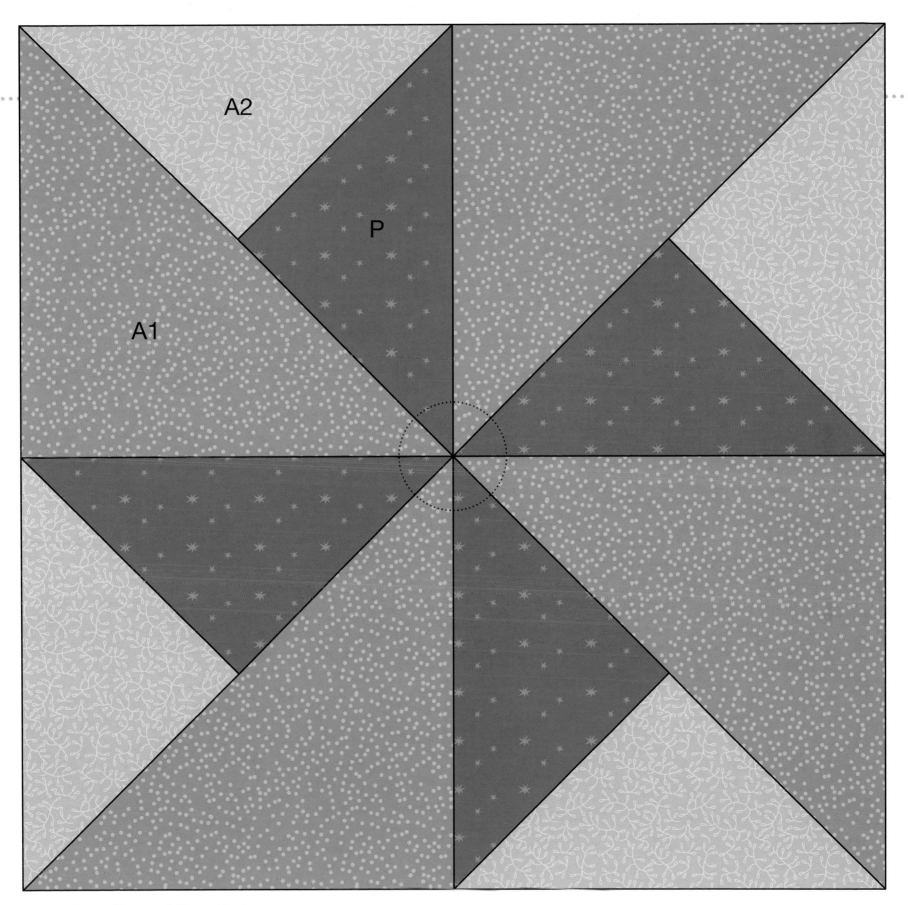

PRAIRIE POINT FLOWER *full-size block*

garden flower

HOW TO CONSTRUCT THIS BLOCK

Make the A section by joining the A pieces in numerical order. Inset the B pieces in the A units. Join the C pieces to the corners of the block. Use stem stitch to embroider stamens on the flower, and a French knot at the end of each stamen.

look again

This simple yet stunning flower shape takes on a geometric effect when it is combined side-by-side, forming diamond shapes between the blocks.

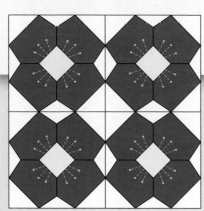

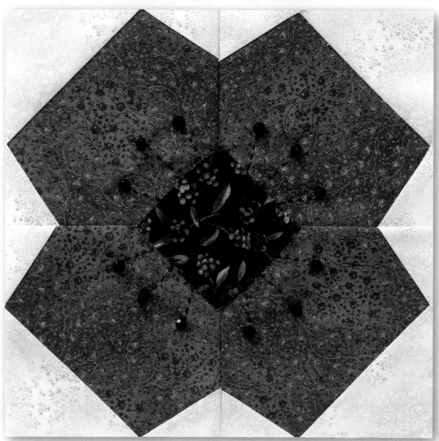

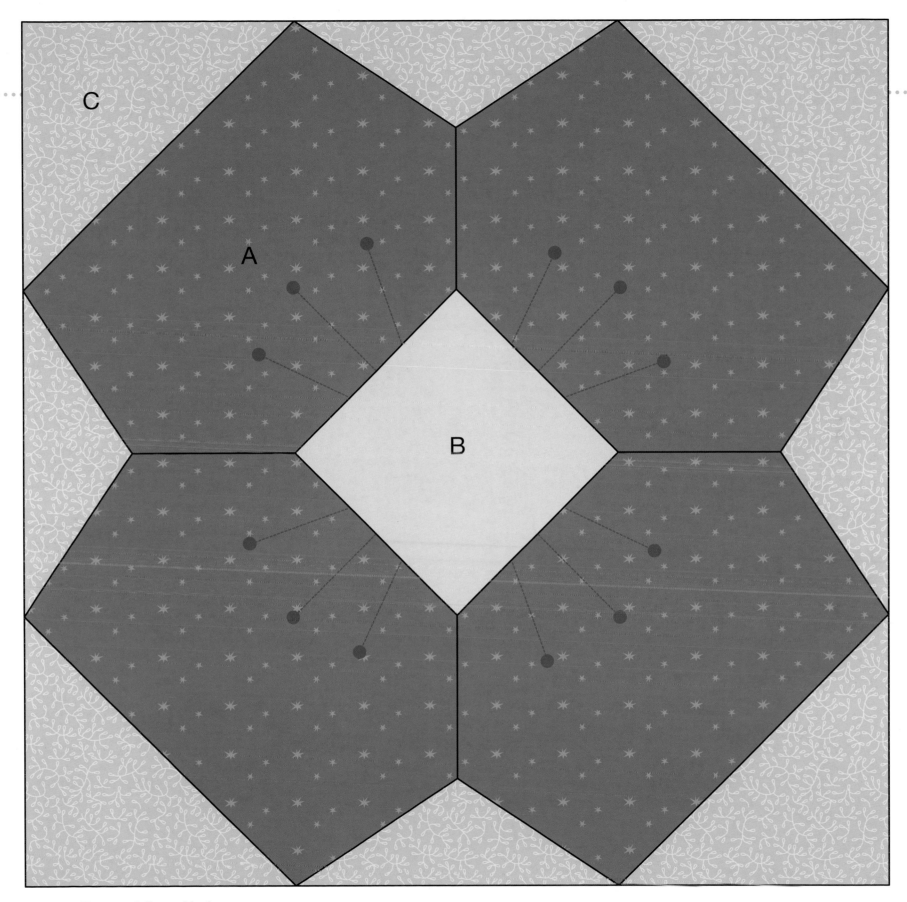

C

A

B

GARDEN FLOWER *full-size block*

tulip bouquet

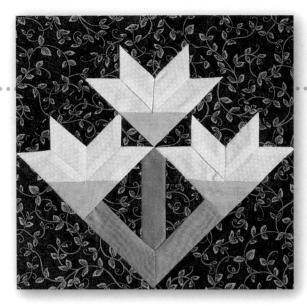

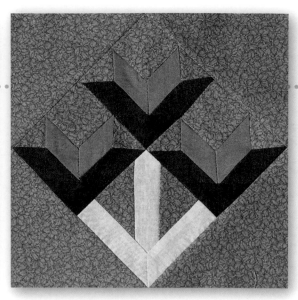

HOW TO CONSTRUCT THIS BLOCK

Sew A to B; stop stitching ¼ inch from end, at the point where B meets Ar. Sew Ar to adjacent edge of B, again stitching to ¼ inch from end. Stitch A and Ar pieces together; repeat 5 more times. Sew C to ABAr unit at Ar edge. Stop stitching ¼ inch from end, at the point where C joins ArA. Stitch a second ABAr unit to adjacent edge of C, stitching to Ar edge. Again stop stitching ¼ inch from end. Sew ArA and ArA together. Sew D to AAr edges; repeat 2 more times. Sew F to each side of E. Sew G to FEF unit; stop stitching ¼ inch from end, at point where E joins GGr. Sew Gr piece to adjacent side of FEF unit, again stitching to ¼ inch from end. Stitch G and Gr together. Sew two flower units together. Sew stem unit to third flower unit, then stitch these two units together. Sew H to each edge of flower block, stitching two opposite sides first, then remaining two sides.

HOW TO MAKE THIS QUILT

This quilt is designed to be a full-size quilt measuring 78½×96½ inches. It uses a 4½-inch-wide solid color border and 3¼-inch-wide Fan border. (See page 210.)

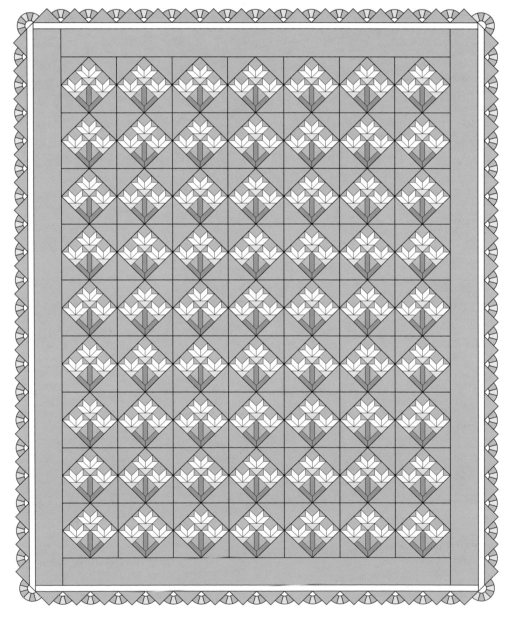

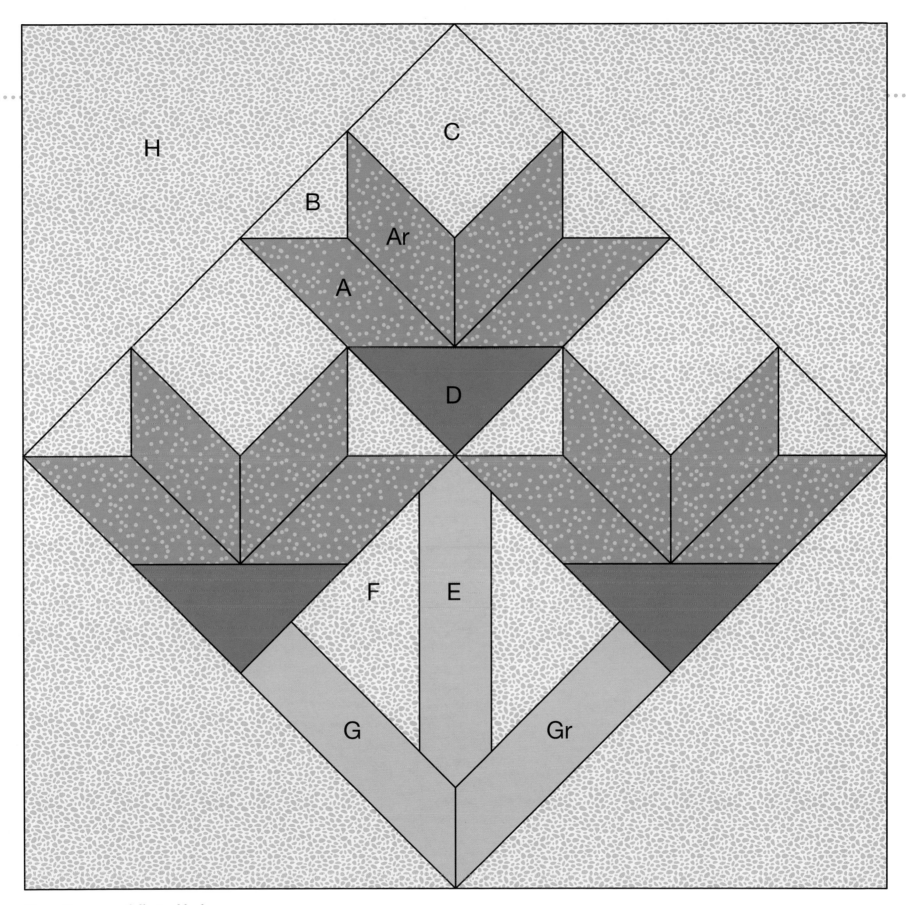

TULIP BOUQUET *full-size block*

posy row

HOW TO CONSTRUCT THIS BLOCK

Sew B to A along one side, stopping at seam allowance of A. Sew B to A (3 more times) in counterclockwise direction. Complete seam for first BA. Sew C to B (4 times) to complete unit 1. Make this unit 1 two times. Sew E and F to opposite sides of D (2 times). Sew Er and F to opposite sides of Dr (2 times). Sew EDF and ErDrF units to opposite sides of G (2 times) to make unit 2 twice. Join four units 1 and 2 to complete block.

HOW TO MAKE THIS QUILT

This quilt is designed to be a queen-size quilt measuring 81×99 inches. It uses the 4½-inch-wide Triangles border (see page 208), and 9-inch setting squares as shown.

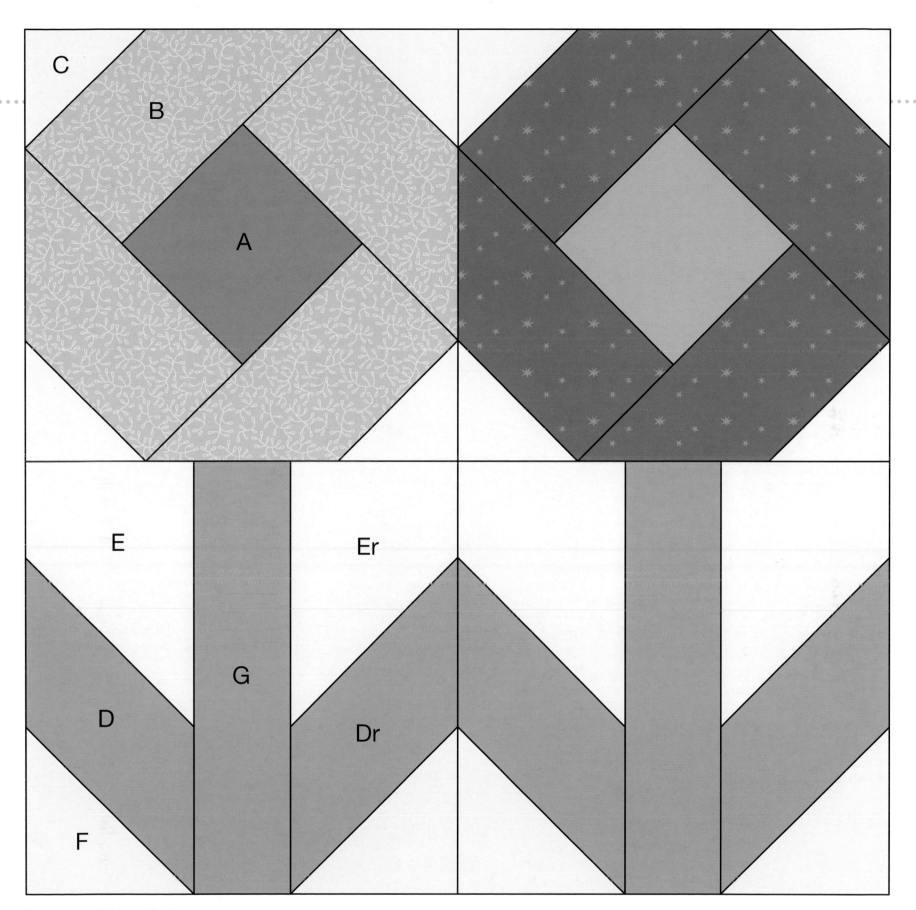

Posy Row *full-size block*

wild rose

HOW TO CONSTRUCT THIS BLOCK

Use lightweight fusible web to appliqué pieces in numerical order. Machine-appliqué edges of all pieces, extending stitching on Q7 pieces to define petals. Make flower stem by machine- or hand-embroidered satin stitch. Use a stem stitch to embroider veins in leaves and stamens, making a French knot at the end of each stamen.

about this block

Appliquéd flowers are always beautiful—many quilt patterns are created by appliquéing the flower from each state onto a block. Another popular embroidered quilt theme is embroidering the bird from each state onto a block and combining these into a finished quilt.

WILD ROSE *full-size block*

flower in the window

HOW TO CONSTRUCT THIS BLOCK

Sew A to A (8 times), making four Four-Patch squares. Sew B to C (4 times). Sew A square to BC (2 times); add A square (2 times). Sew D to E; add D. Sew DED to F. Sew G to H and G to Hr. Set in GH and GHr to each side of DEDF. Sew I to J and I to Jr; add K (2 times). Sew IJK and I JrK to each side of center unit. Sew BC to each side of center unit. Sew ABC to top and bottom of center unit. Satin-stitch flower detail and use a stem stitch between leaves.

HOW TO MAKE THIS QUILT

This quilt is designed to be a full-size quilt measuring 78×102 inches. It uses a 4½-inch-wide solid color border, 3-inch-wide sashing strips, and setting squares as shown. A Four-Patch block is added in each corner of the border.

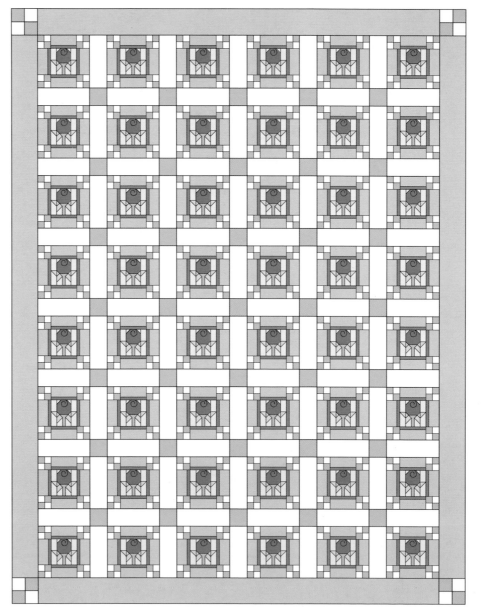

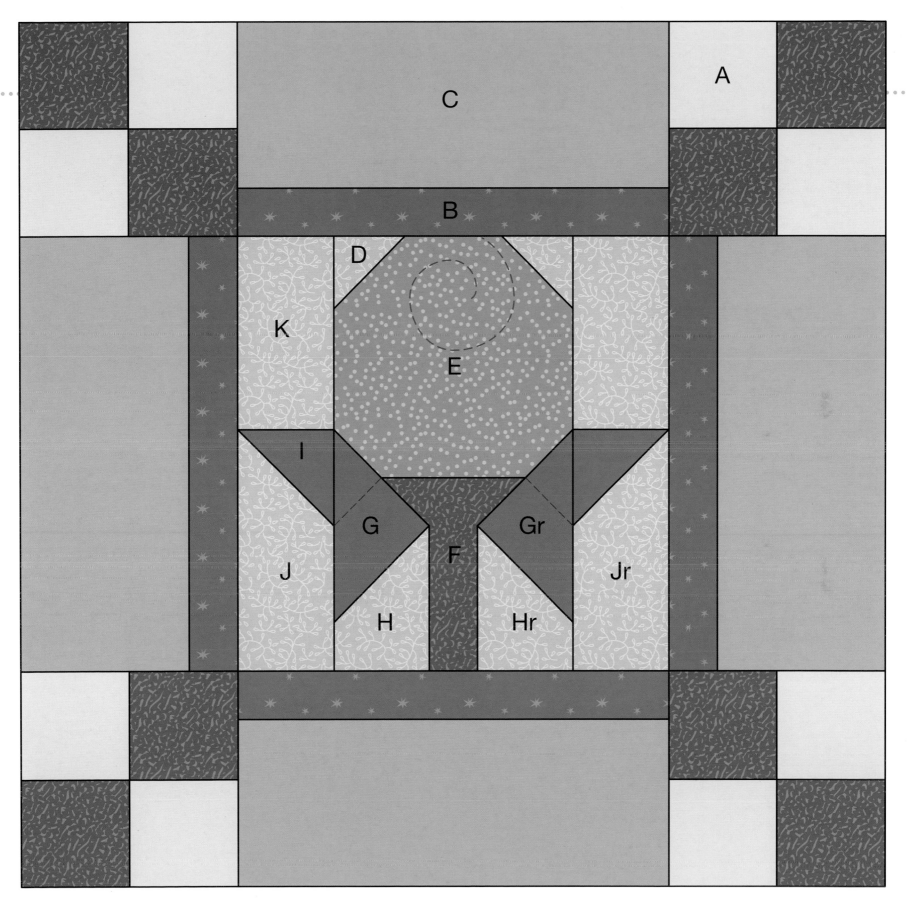

Flower in the Window *full-size block*

flowers four

HOW TO CONSTRUCT THIS BLOCK

Sew A to A (8 times). Sew AA to AA (4 times). Sew B to AAAA (4 times); add C (4 times). Sew AABC to D; add AABC (2 times). Sew three Ds together. Sew three rows together. Appliqué E, overlap F, and appliqué. Add G and then H. Finish appliqué edges using blanket stitches if desired.

HOW TO MAKE THIS QUILT

This quilt is designed to be a twin-size quilt measuring 69×93 inches. It uses a 3-inch-wide Checkerboard border (see page 213), 3-inch-wide sashing strips, and pieced setting blocks as shown.

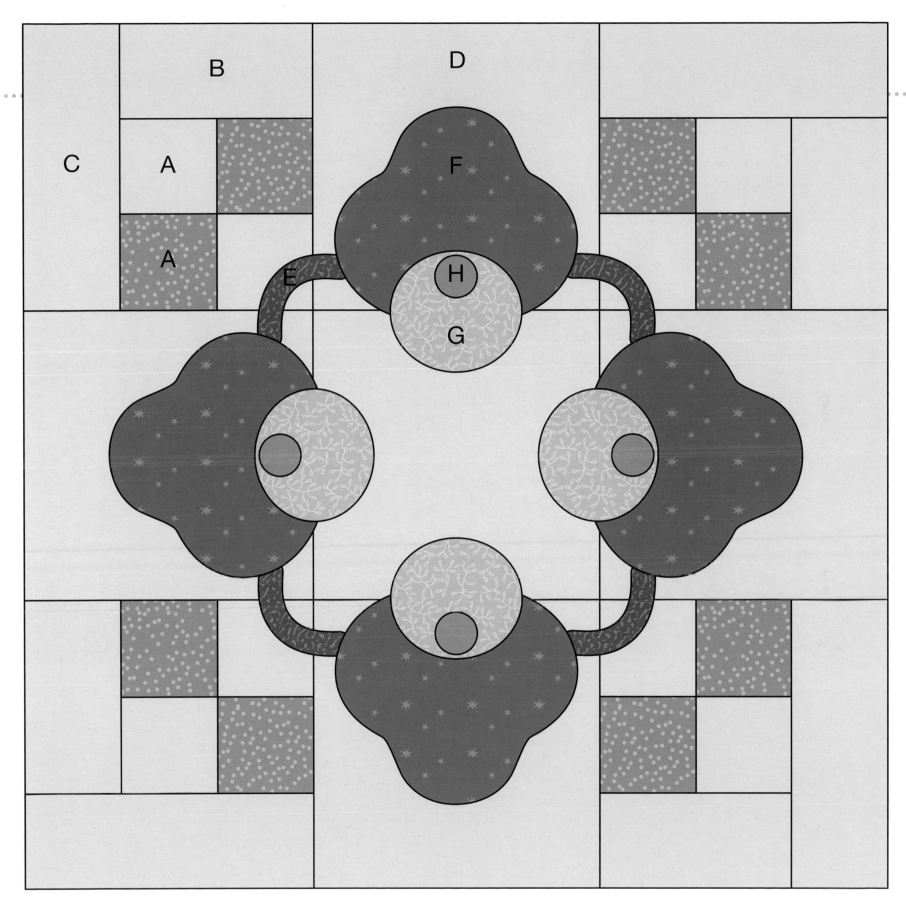

FLOWERS FOUR *full-size block*

dogwood

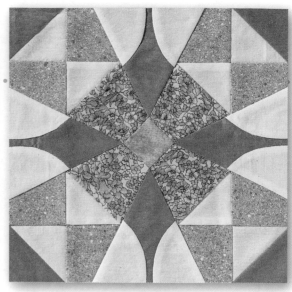

HOW TO CONSTRUCT THIS BLOCK

Sew two E pieces together (4 times). Sew D to EE (4 times). Sew C to Dr (4 times). Combine CDr and EED (4 times) to make CDE unit. Sew B to CDE unit (4 times). Sew F and Fr to G (4 times). Sew FGFr to each side of BCDE (2 times). Sew A to BCDE unit (2 times). Join the top and bottom units to the center section.

HOW TO MAKE THIS QUILT

This quilt is designed to be a twin-size quilt measuring 75×93 inches. It uses a 1½-inch-wide solid color border with mitered corners as shown.

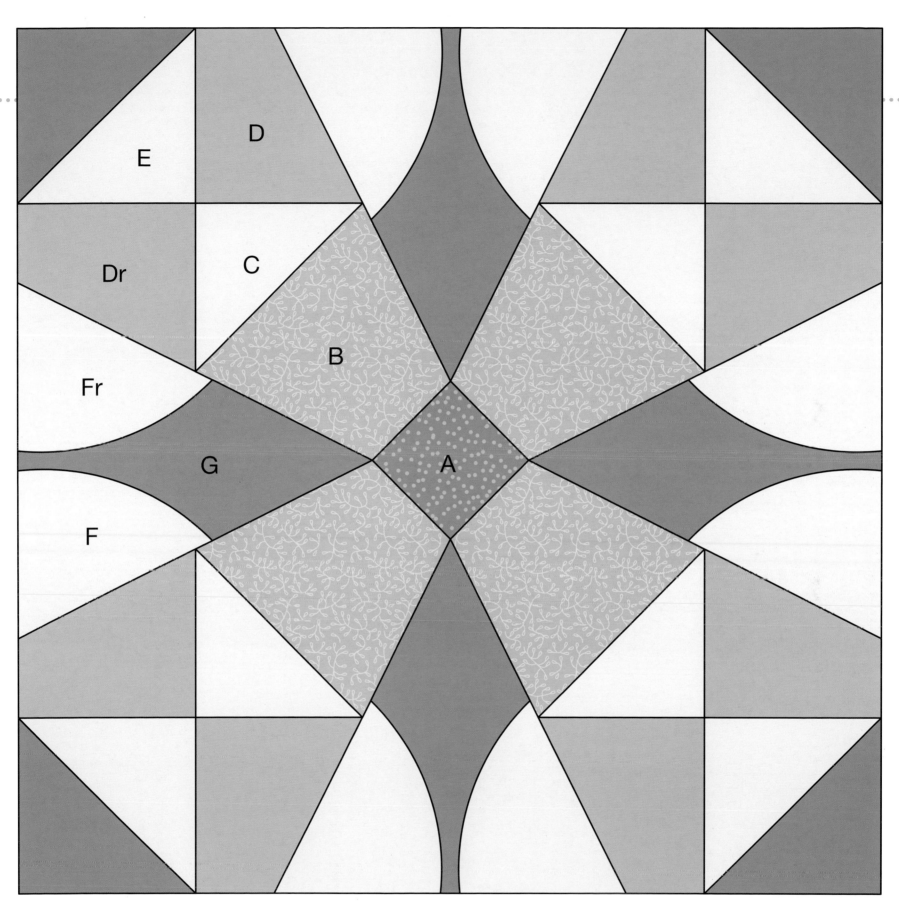

Dogwood *full-size block*

vintage
classics

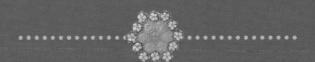

Vintage quilt block patterns such as
Anvil, Tree of Life, Shoo Fly, and Jacob's
Ladder inspire quilters with their classic beauty.
These designs will find their way into the hearts
of quilters for generations to come.

INSPIRATION

In the early 1800s, both pieced and appliquéd quilts were frequently made in a medallion style. These quilts had a center design surrounded by borders.

The first patchwork designs were simple geometric patterns based on the most basic shapes—the square and the right triangle. A few complicated star designs and circular Mariner's Compass patterns were devised by very accomplished stitchers.

Early quilts abound with stars, pinwheels, flowers, and borders of appliquéd vines and swags, themes evident in earlier needlework forms.

The roots of the classic quilting designs used today are found in colonial quilts. Plain grids and parallel lines, as well as fancy flowers and undulating feathers are seen on the earliest surviving wholecloth quilts.

As the 19th century began, America had its own cloth industry. The first cotton textile plant opened in 1790 at Pawtucket, Rhode Island. The resulting flood of inexpensive and washable cottons unleashed a new creativity in quiltmaking that came to be the American patchwork quilt. Structured designs of patchwork emerged as the 1800s began. Nine-Patch, Pinwheel, Sawtooth Star, and Flying Geese are some of the earliest patterns. The early American quiltmaker arranged basic geometric shapes from the patterns seen in stenciling, architecture, weaving, and the starry skies and furrowed field of the countryside.

After 1800, quiltmaking became more widespread and quiltmakers developed a new concept—the use of small individual blocks. Blocks made one at a time and joined together were practical, yet still met the maker's need for order and beauty.

Block patterns were designed through quilting bees, prolific letters, and itinerant peddlers and began to travel across the country. In each region, a block acquired new names and variations, often commemorating important people or events. This is how the classic Robbing

ABOVE *A flow blue china plate from the 1890s offers similar color and design style as many quilts of the time.*

Peter to Pay Paul block also came to be known as Dolley Madison's Workbox.

Classic quilt block patterns such as Shoo Fly, Prairie Queen, Anvil, and Goosetracks are a few of the hundreds of classic quilt patterns that found their way across America.

LEFT *Exquisite book covers from the 1800s and early 1900s inspire the use of fine line quilting or embellishments on handmade quilts of the same time period.* RIGHT *A child's tiny tin pitcher with a Sunbonnet Baby on the side is a well-worn toy of long ago.*

geese in the corner

HOW TO CONSTRUCT THIS BLOCK

Sew B to C and Br to Cr. Sew BC to BrCr. Set in A to BC; stop the stitching at the seam line. Reposition A and begin stitching at the seam line. Be careful not to stitch through the BBr seam. Sew E to each short side of D (8 times). Stitch four EDE units together (2 times). Sew two Fs together (2 times). Join together to make a Four-Patch unit. Sew one EDE unit to the right side of ABrCr. Sew one EDE unit to the Four-Patch unit and join it to the bottom of the ABCEDE unit.

HOW TO MAKE THIS QUILT

This quilt is designed to be a king-size quilt measuring 93×114 inches, including 3-inch-wide sashing strips with Four-Patch block sashing squares. The plain inner border is 3 inches wide and the outer 3-inch-wide Flying Geese border with Four-Patch corners is taken from the block as shown.

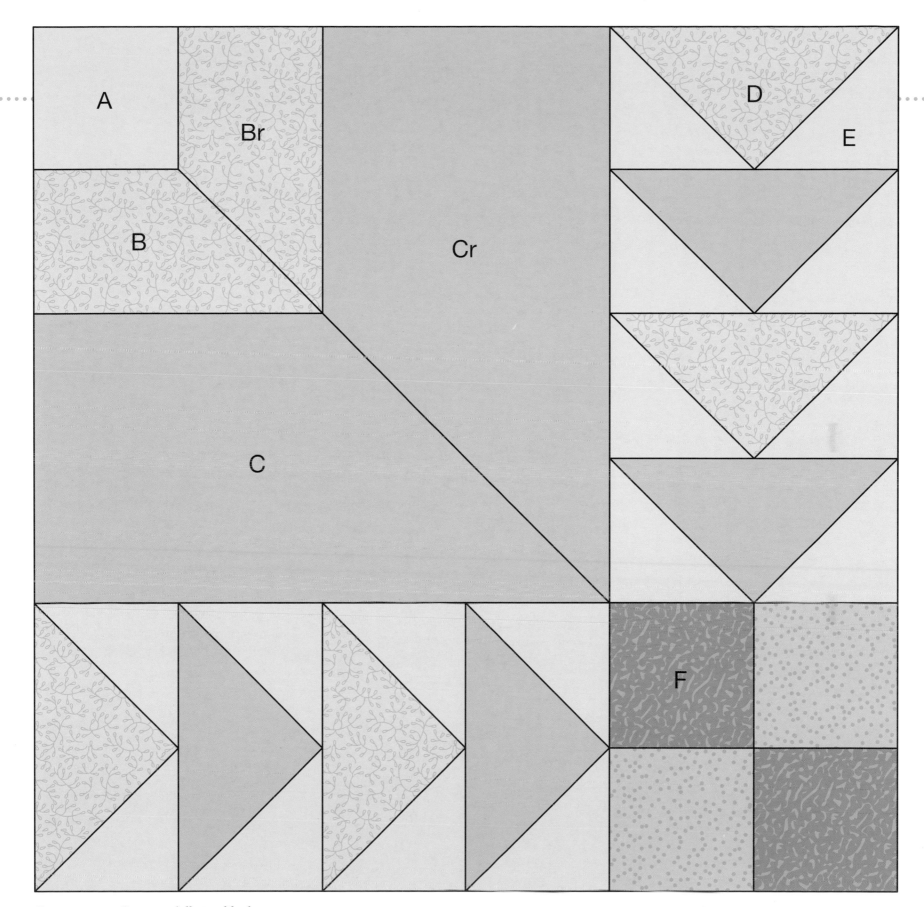

GEESE IN THE CORNER *full-size block*

jacob's ladder variation

HOW TO CONSTRUCT
THIS BLOCK

Make AA unit (6 times). Make BBB
unit (9 times); combine three BBB
units to make a Nine-Patch (3 times).
(See directions for Nine-Patch on page
214.) Sew two AA units with Nine-
Patch on one end (2 times) for top and
bottom strips. Sew two AA units with
Nine-Patch in the center for center
strip. Sew top and bottom strips to
center strip.

HOW TO MAKE
THIS QUILT

This quilt is designed to be a queen-
size square quilt measuring 91×91
inches. We have used a 2-inch-wide
solid color border, a 3-inch-wide
Checkerboard border (see page 213),
3-inch-wide sashing strips, and setting
squares as shown.

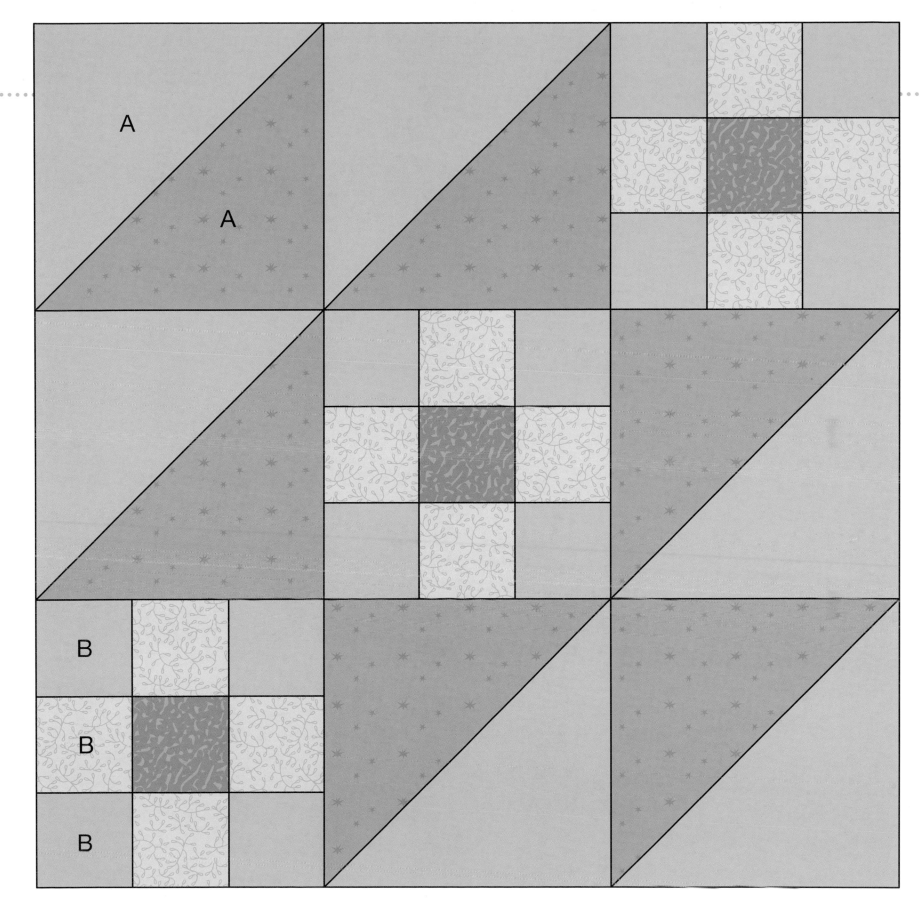

Jacob's Ladder Variation *full-size block*

squares in the corner

HOW TO CONSTRUCT THIS BLOCK

Make the A section by joining the A pieces. Make the B and C sections. Join the B section to the A section. Join the C section to the A B unit.

look again

This geometric block is excellent for showcasing a favorite conversation fabric in the center. Placing several blocks together wll create a linked appearance and can tell a story by the choice of fabric in the center. The block is also a good choice for a signature block.

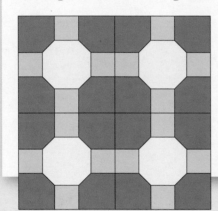

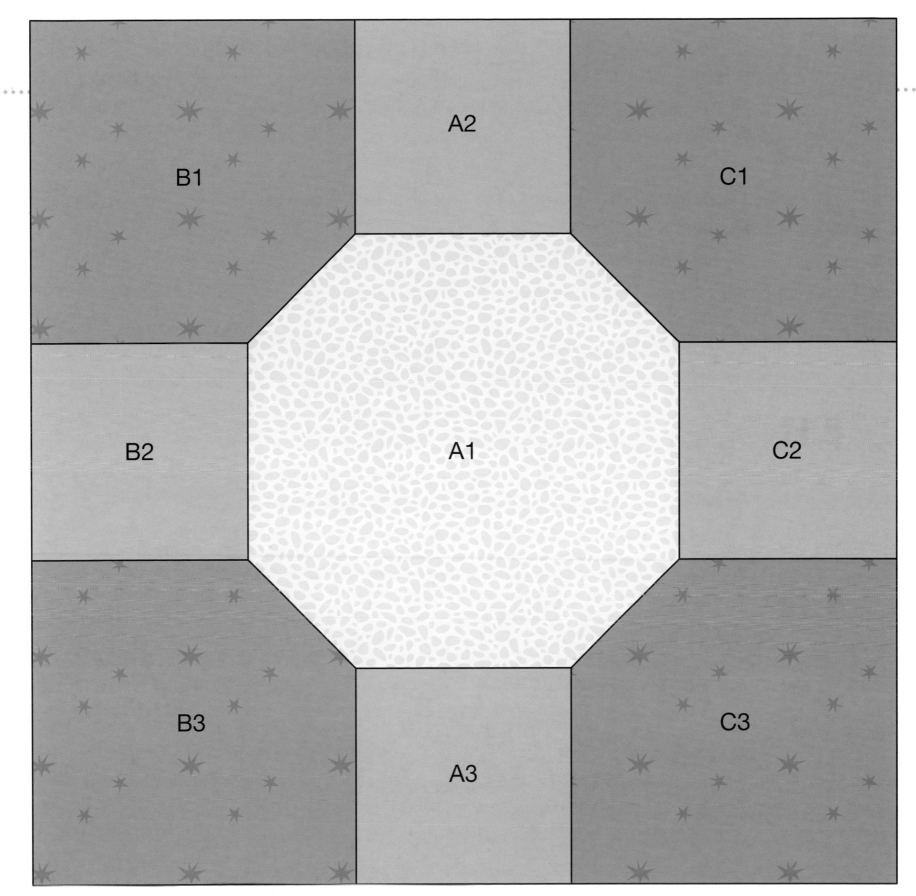

Squares in the Corner *full-size block*

tree of life

HOW TO CONSTRUCT THIS BLOCK
Make DD unit (28 times). Sew G to H, and G to Hr; add each unit to F. Join FGH with E pieces to complete trunk section. Assemble DD units with C, A, and B pieces to make the 3 top rows and join the rows into top section. Make left section in 4 vertical rows and join the rows. For right section, add a row of DD units to trunk section. Join the left and right sections, then add to top section to complete the block.

about this block

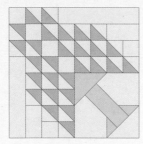

The Tree of Life block is an early quilt block pattern that is said to have a biblical reference, as did many names of that time. The reference to the tree of life comes from Genesis, Chapter 2. This beloved pattern is oftentimes pieced using just two colors, although using colors from the same color family gives the tree pattern more dimension.

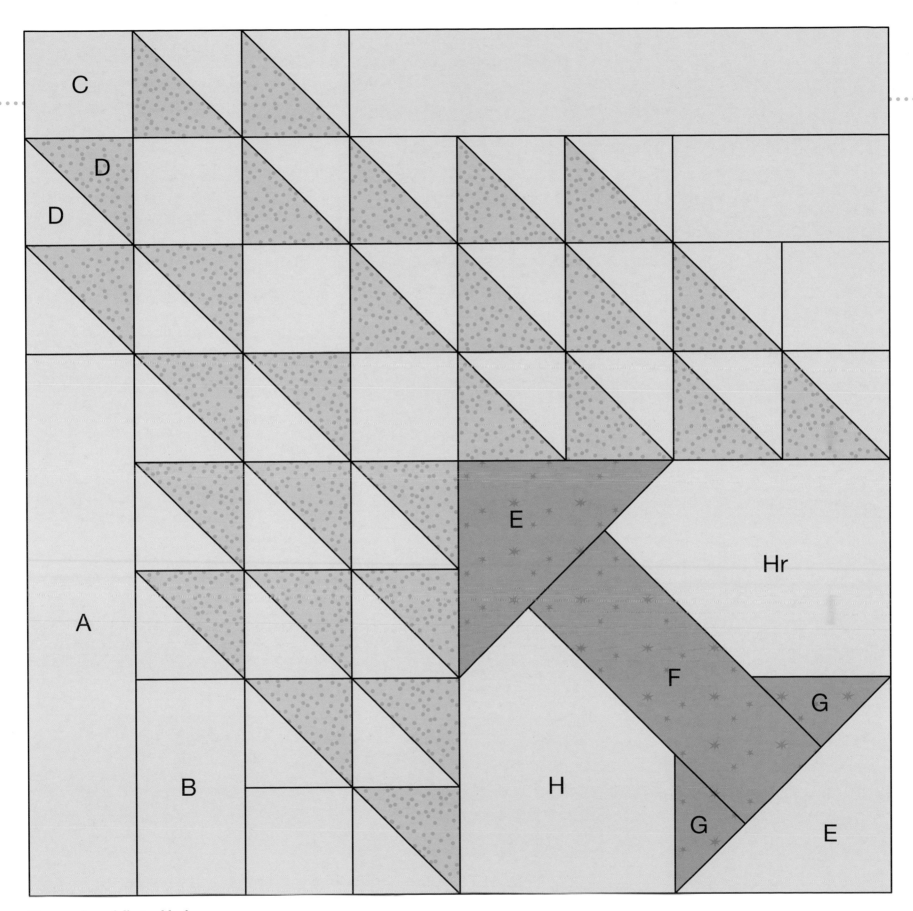

T<small>REE OF</small> L<small>IFE</small> *full-size block*

diamond five

HOW TO CONSTRUCT THIS BLOCK

Mark B, C, and D with center guideline marks. To join the pieces, use a pin to match the marks. Stitch B to C (4 times). Add D (4 times). Stitch F to two sides of E (4 times). Sew EFF to opposite sides of BCD (2 times). Sew BCD to opposite sides of A. Stitch BCDEFF to opposite sides of ABCD.

HOW TO MAKE THIS QUILT

This quilt is designed to be a twin-size quilt measuring 76½×103½ inches. The blocks are set on point with setting triangles bordering the blocks. The inner border is 2¾ inches at the top and bottom and 2 inches at the sides. The 4½-inch outer border is Diamond Link from page 210.

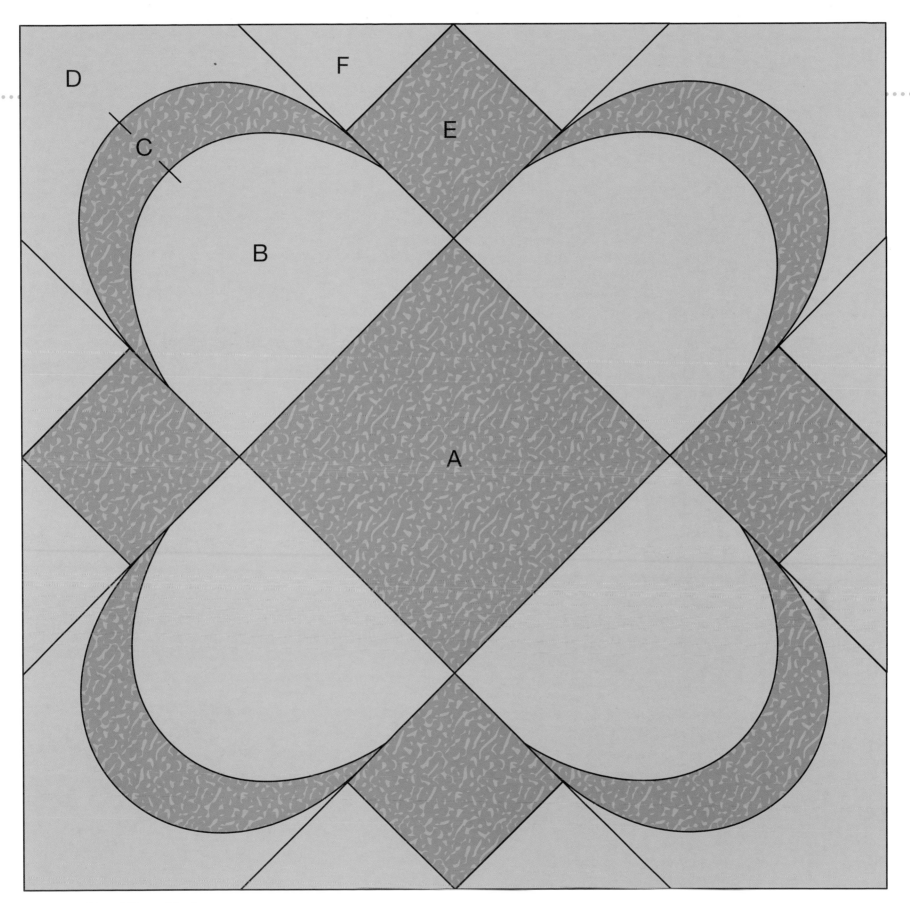

D

F

C

E

B

A

DIAMOND FIVE *full-size block*

prairie queen

HOW TO CONSTRUCT THIS BLOCK

Sew light A to dark A (8 times). Sew AA to AA, reversing color placement (4 times). Sew light B to dark B (4 times). Sew BB to AAAA; add BB (2 times) for Rows 1 and 3. Sew AAAA to C; add AAAA for Row 2. Stitch Row 1 to Row 2; add Row 3.

HOW TO MAKE THIS QUILT

This quilt is designed to be a twin-size quilt measuring 72×90 inches. A 4-inch border with alternating triangles completes the quilt.

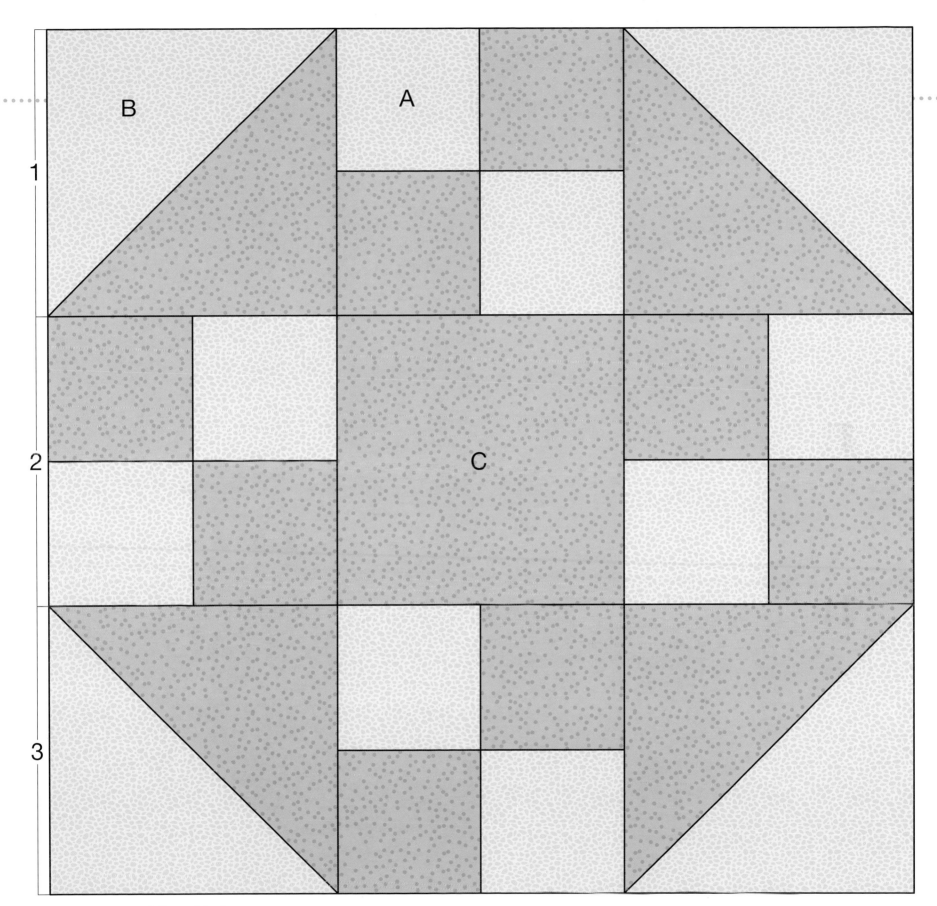

B

A

C

PRAIRIE QUEEN *full-size block*

crossroads

HOW TO CONSTRUCT THIS BLOCK

Make 4 A sections. Join A units with D pieces to make
2 A D units. Join B and C pieces to make 2 B C units.
Join the 4 units to complete the block.

look again

This easy-to-piece block takes on a stunning look
in *when it is combined with identical blocks that are*
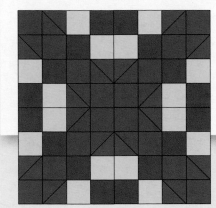
*rotated to form
a new and
surprisingly
graphic shape in
the center of the
group of four.*

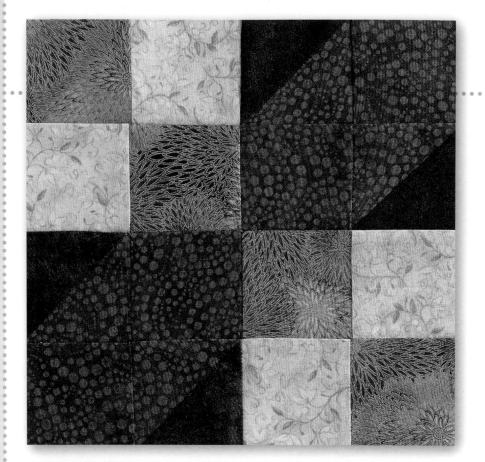

CROSSROADS *full-size block*

anvil

HOW TO CONSTRUCT THIS BLOCK

Make 2 A sections by joining the A pieces in numerical order. Make 2 B sections. Join the C1 and C2 pieces. Join a B section to each side of the C section. Join the A sections to the top and bottom of the B-C-B unit.

look again

Combining this vintage block in a group of four makes a very geometric and traditional look as well as a pleasing design. By changing the lights and darks in a more random fashion, the blocks will create a less geometric and more unexpected appearance.

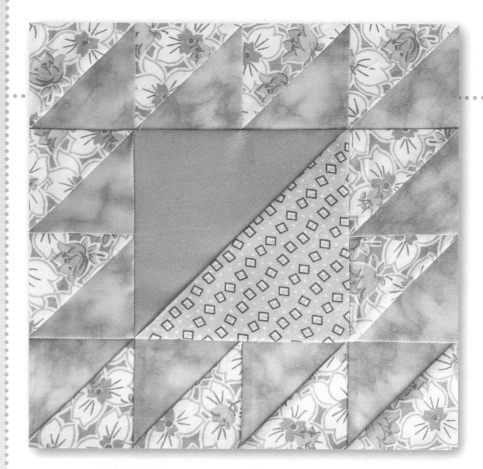

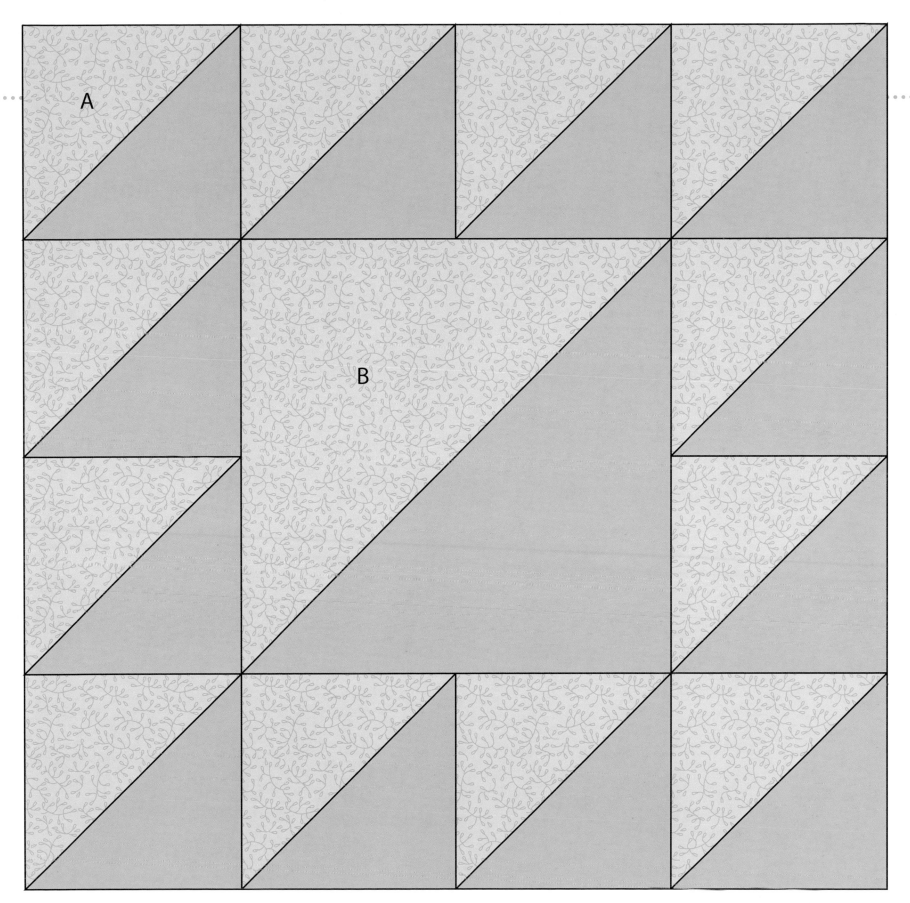

ANVIL *full-size block*

pretty bow

HOW TO CONSTRUCT THIS BLOCK

Make the A section by joining the A pieces in numerical order. Make the B section and join to the A section. Make the C section and join to the A B unit. Make the D section and join to the A B C unit. Make a fabric yo-yo and attach to the center of bow.

about this block

This pretty bow block seems almost three-dimensional because of the yo-yo center.
To add interest and dimension to any favorite block, make a yo-yo to add to the block. Very popular in the early 1900s, yo-yos are made using a circle of fabric. To determine the cutting size of the yo-yo piece, determine the finished size of the yo-yo and double the diameter. Then run a gathering stitch around the edge and pull together to form the yo-yo.

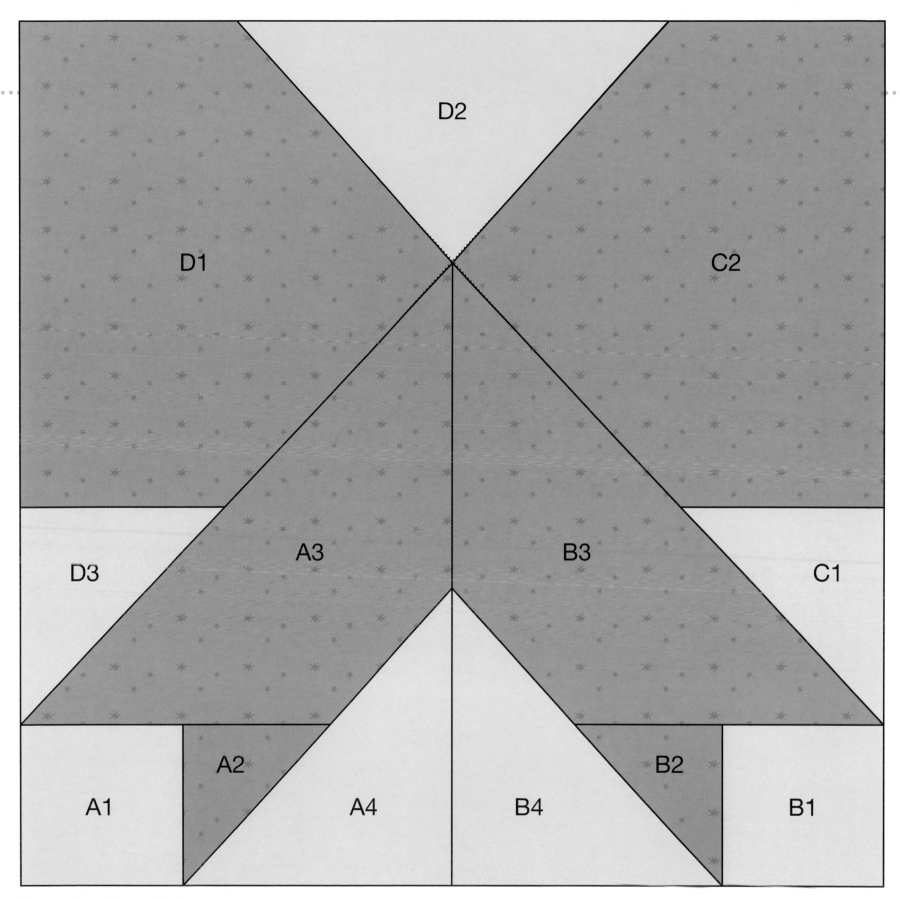

PRETTY BOW *full-size block*

shoo fly

HOW TO CONSTRUCT THIS BLOCK

Sew A to A (4 times). Sew AA to opposite sides of dark B (2 times), being careful of placement for Rows 1 and 3. Sew dark B to opposite sides of light B for Row 2. Sew Row 1 to Row 2; add Row 3.

HOW TO MAKE THIS QUILT

This quilt is designed to be a queen-size quilt measuring 95×112 inches. The blocks are set on point, and setting triangles finish the quilt center. The sashing consists of three 1-inch-wide strips with 3-inch squares. The border is 3 inches wide.

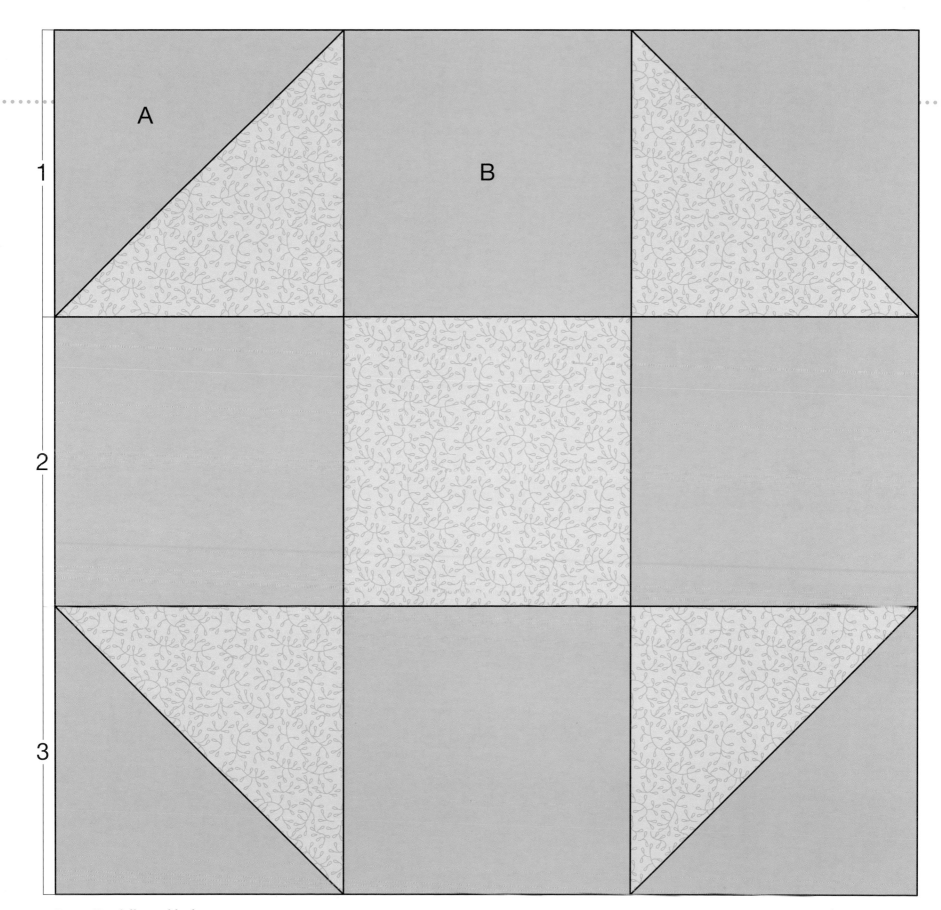

SHOO FLY *full-size block*

hearts and gizzards

HOW TO CONSTRUCT
THIS BLOCK

Cut four A triangles from one color.
Cut four A triangles from a second
color. Appliqué two matching Bs onto
opposite color A (8 times). Sew two
A (opposite color) triangles to make
a square (4 times). Sew two squares
together (2 times). Sew the two pieced
rectangles together to make a block.

HOW TO MAKE
THIS QUILT

This quilt is designed to be a twin-size
quilt measuring 66×75 inches. It uses
two 3-inch-wide solid color mitered
borders as shown.

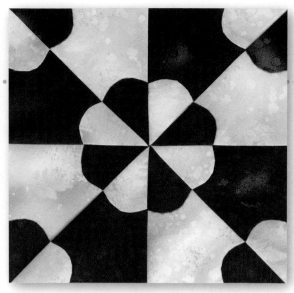

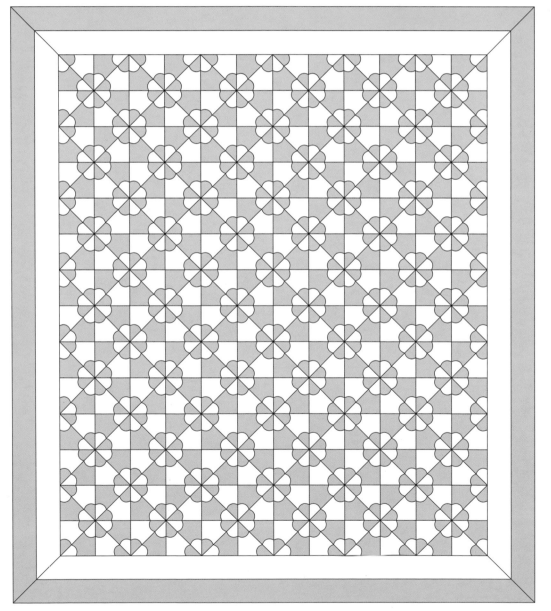

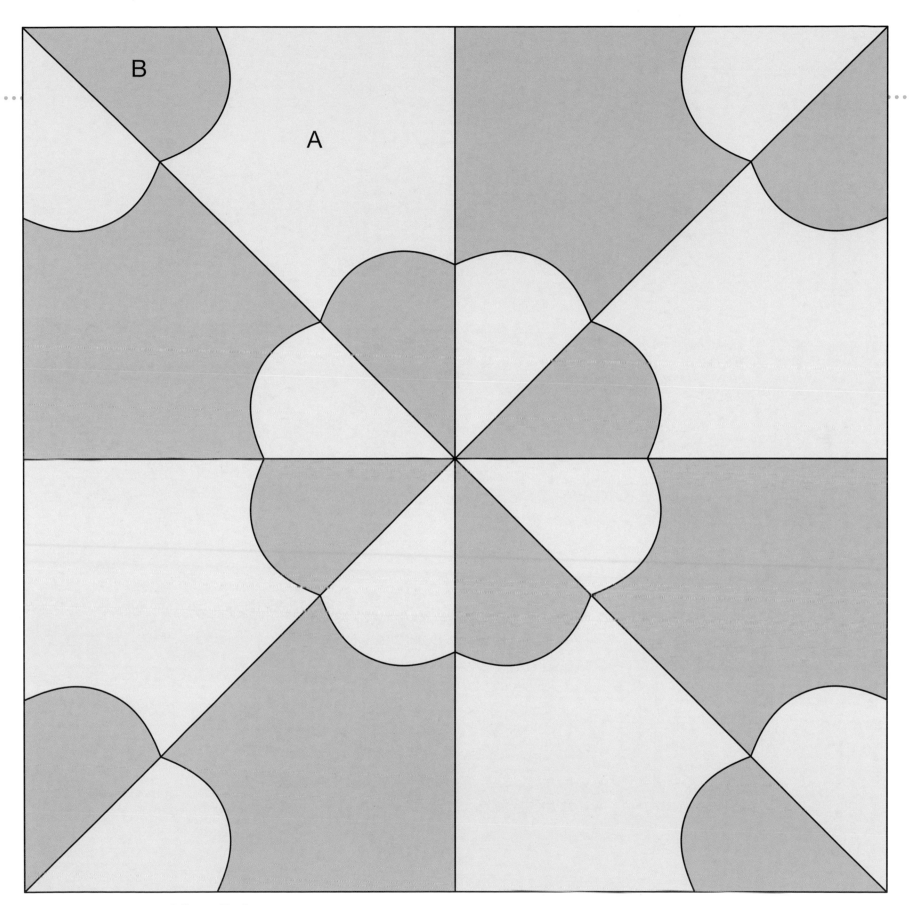

HEARTS AND GIZZARDS *full-size block*

basket variation

HOW TO CONSTRUCT THIS BLOCK

Sew A to A (5 times). Sew three AA units together; add A. Sew two AA units together; add A. Sew C to 2AA. Add A. Sew C2AA,A to 3AA,A to make Unit 1. Sew B to each side of Unit 1. Sew E to each side of D. Sew EDE to Unit 1. Sew F to G and Gr. Sew GFGr to Unit 1.

HOW TO MAKE THIS QUILT

This quilt is designed to be a full-size quilt measuring 83x83 inches. We have used a solid color 1-inch-wide border to finish the quilt.

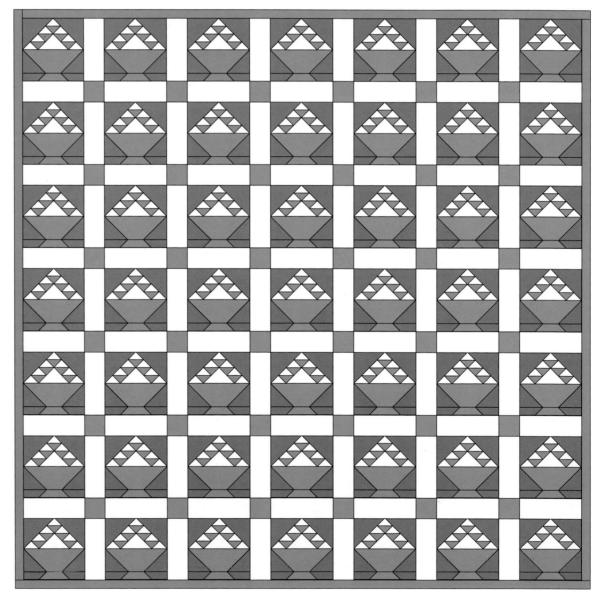

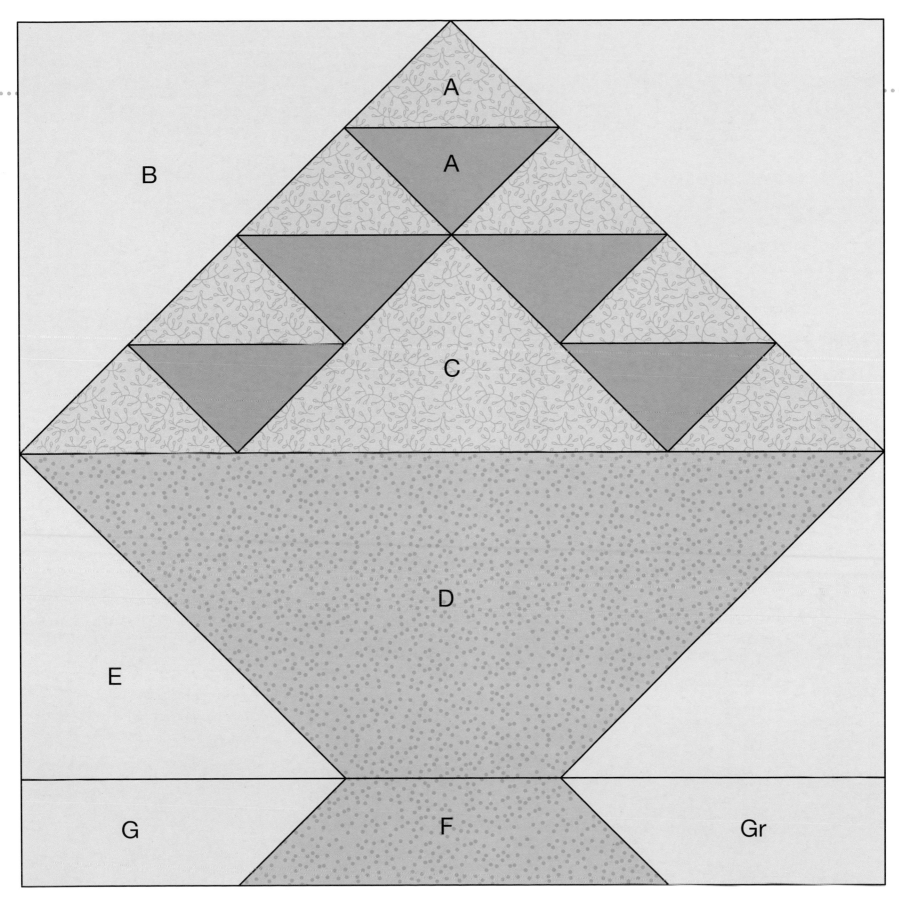

Basket Variation *full-size block*

fan blades

HOW TO CONSTRUCT THIS BLOCK

Make the A section by joining the A pieces in numerical order. Make the B section and join to the A section. Make the C section and join to the A-B unit. Make the D section and join to the A B C unit. Make the E and F sections and join together. Join the E F unit to the A B C D unit.

look again

This lively block becomes even more fun when it is sewn together with identical blocks. The placement of color and pattern are key to the spinning look of the finished quilt.

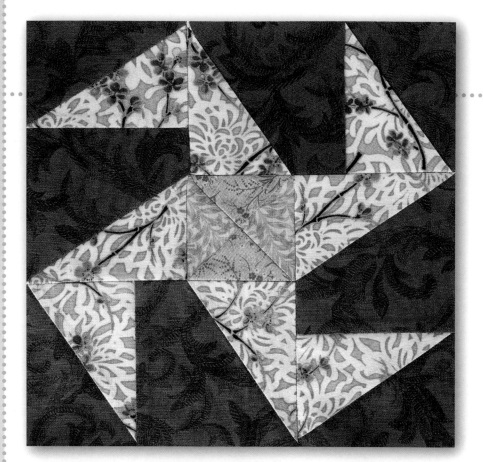

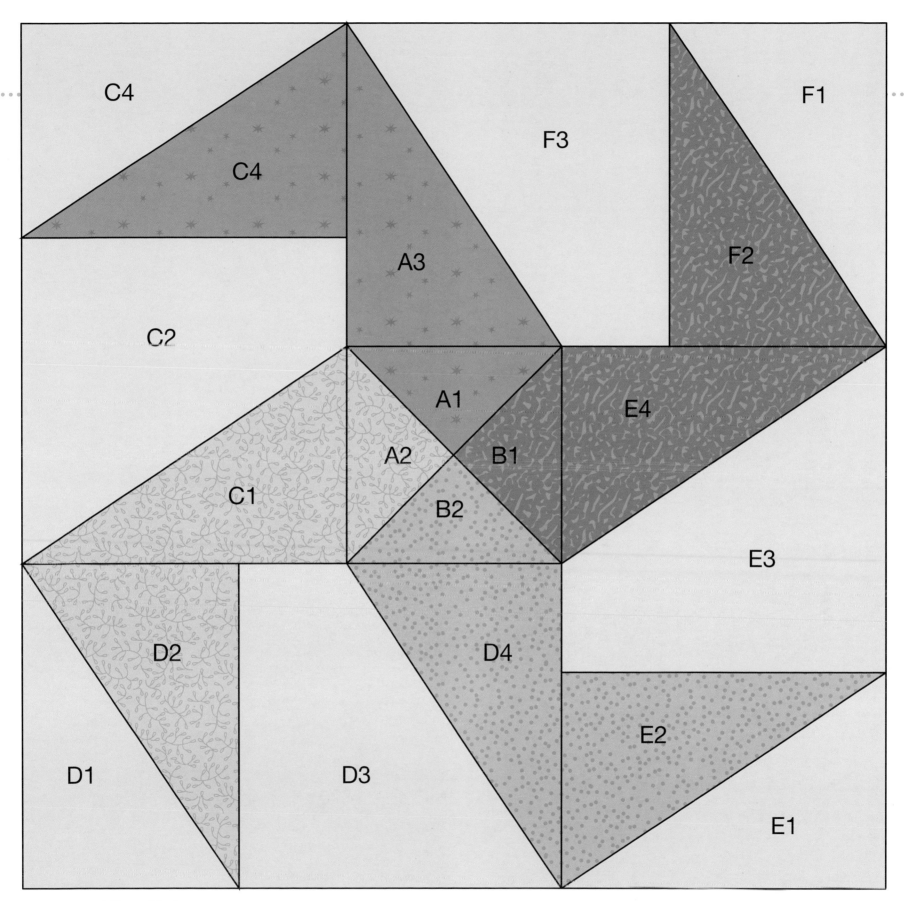

Fan Blades *full-size block*

basket weave

HOW TO CONSTRUCT THIS BLOCK

This block can be made by sewing strips together, then cutting them apart into squares, and then sewing the squares together, (see page 215 for strip piecing instructions). Or, each unit can be sewn individually, using the A template: Make AAA unit (16 times). Sew units together into rows, then sew rows together to make the block.

look again

The look of the finished quilt changes dramatically with the placement of the lights and darks in the block.

Even though the blocks are straightforward to make, the finished quilt can take on a completely new look each time.

A

BASKET WEAVE *full-size block*

drunkard's path

HOW TO CONSTRUCT THIS BLOCK

Make 16 AB units. (See page 214 for help with sewing curved seams.) Sew the AB units into rows, then sew the rows together to make the block.

look again

A favorite pattern with a variety of names, Drunkard's Path is often pieced with two solid colors. Other names include "Rocky Road to California" and "Country Husband." Women created quilts using the Drunkard's Path block as a symbol of support for the temperance movement. The finished quilts were sometimes used to raise money for the various temperance groups of the time.

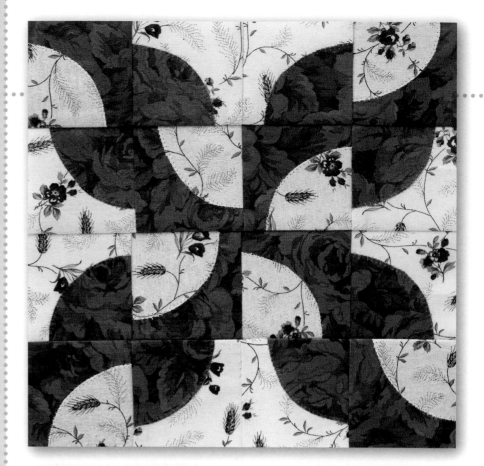

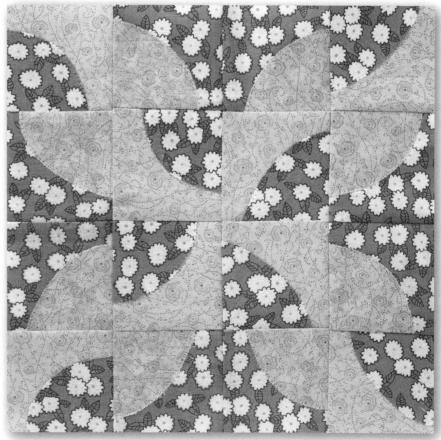

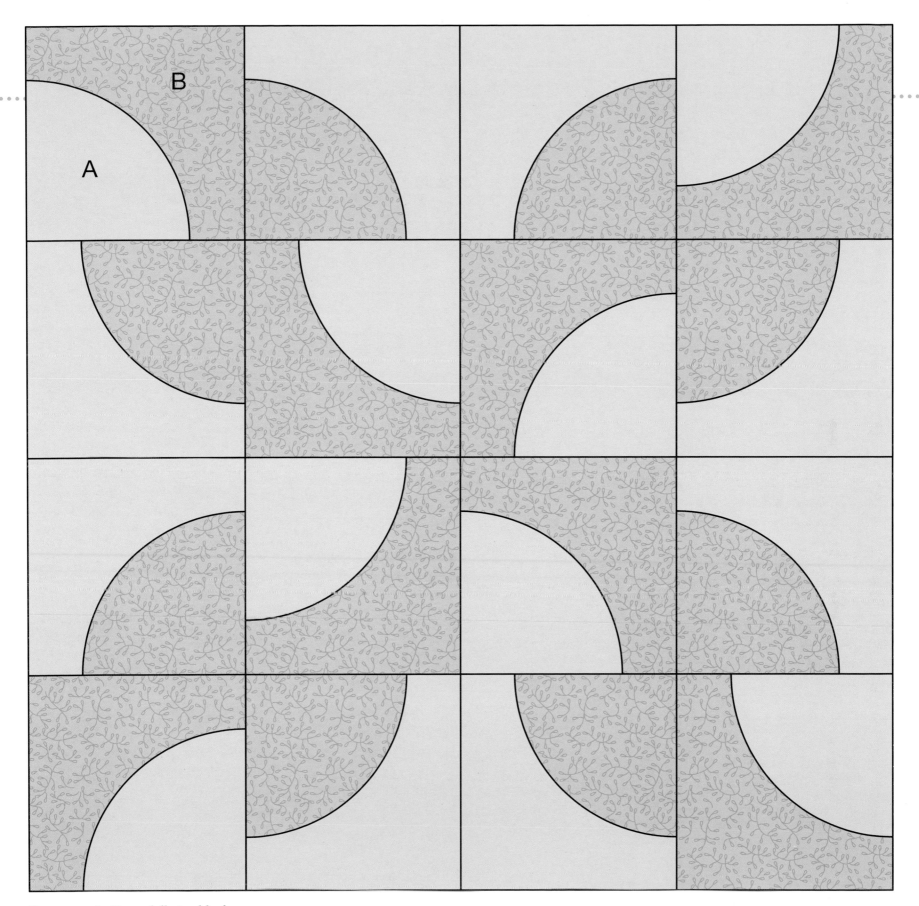

DRUNKARD'S PATH *full-size block*

sunbonnet with purse

HOW TO CONSTRUCT THIS BLOCK

After you appliqué all pieces in place, embroider around the shapes and in the folds on the hat and dress with a stem stitch and blanket stitch (see page 214).

about this block

Sunbonnet Sue was created by artist Bertha L. Corbett in the early 1900s. The artist created the little girl by featuring her with a large summer sunbonnet rather than any facial features.

Corbett drew many Sunbonnet Babies in various poses that appeared in other printed material such as comic strips and advertising.

SUNBONNET WITH PURSE *full-size block*

country boy

HOW TO CONSTRUCT THIS BLOCK

Appliqué figures onto background fabric. Stem stitch bucket handle. After you appliqué all pieces in place, embroider around the shapes with a blanket stitch if desired (see page 214).

about this block

While Sunbonnet Sue may have been the most recognized character that artist Bertha L. Corbett created, the character also had other friends. The Sunbonnet Babies included her friend Overall Sam, sometimes known as Country Boy. This little character always had a straw hat and appeared with his little country favorites such as geese, kittens, dogs, or outdoor toys.

COUNTRY BOY *full-size block*

goosetracks

HOW TO CONSTRUCT THIS BLOCK

Sew light A to dark Ar (4 times). Sew dark A to light Ar (4 times). Sew light AAr to dark AAr (4 times); add B (4 times). Set in C to AArB unit (8 times). Stop the stitching at the seam line of AAr. Reposition C and begin stitching at the seam line. Set in D to AArBC (4 times). Stop the stitching at ArA. Reposition D and begin stitching at the seam line. Sew E to the right side of AArBCD (2 times). Sew the left side of AArBCD to AArBCDE (2 times) to make Rows 1 and 3. Sew a short side of E to F; add E to make Row 2. Stitch Row 1 to Row 2; add Row 3.

HOW TO MAKE THIS QUILT

This quilt is designed to be a queen-size quilt measuring 94½ x107¼ inches. The quilt center blocks are set on point with 4 ½-inch-wide sashing and setting squares. The outer triangles are one-half of the block on point. These triangles need to have the seam allowance added. The border is 9 inches wide with corner blocks.

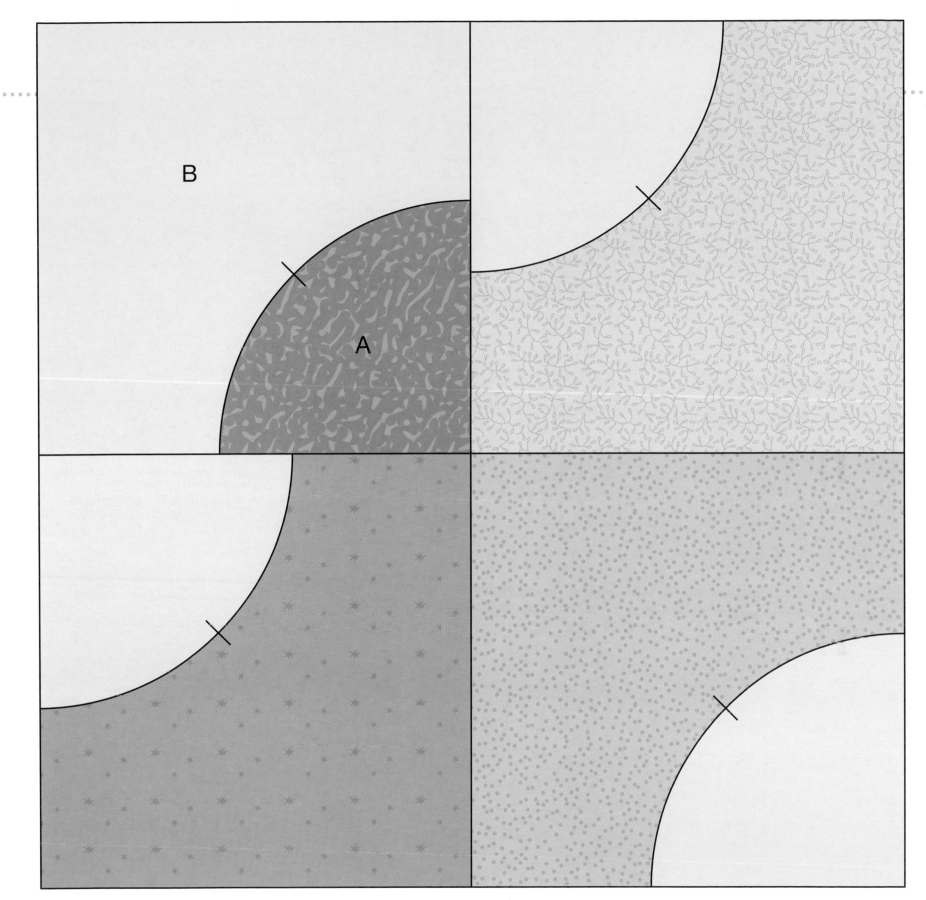

FOOL'S PUZZLE *full-size block*

log cabin

HOW TO CONSTRUCT THIS BLOCK

In this block the letters refer to the template, and the numbers refer to the order in which the pieces are added. Begin in the center (A1); add A2, then B3. Keep adding pieces in this manner through H13.

look again

A perennial favorite, this block can vary greatly with the placement of the fabric and the lights and darks. By grouping the lights on one side and the darks on

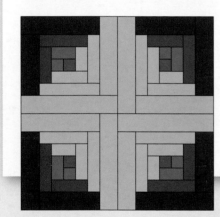

the other, the traditional log cabin look is achieved. When pieced together, a multitude of designs can emerge.

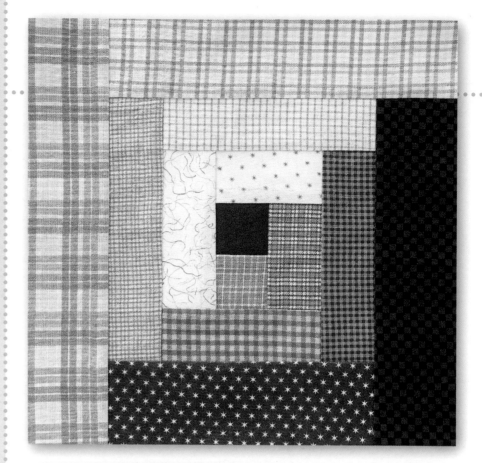

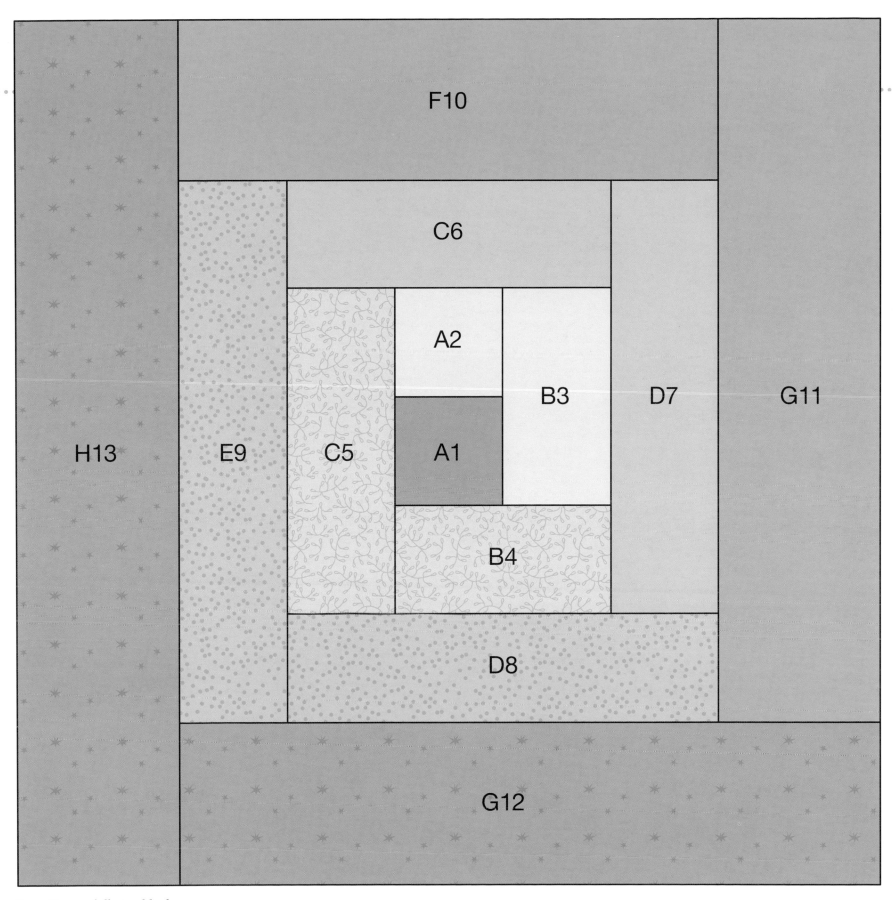

Log Cabin *full-size block*

dresden plate

HOW TO CONSTRUCT THIS BLOCK

Sew A to A (4 times). Sew AA to AA (2 times). Sew AAAA to AAAA. Fold a 10-inch background square in quarters, pressing the lines. Position the A unit onto the background square, matching the seam lines to the pressed lines of the square. Appliqué in place using blanket stitches or other embroidery stitches (see page 214 for stitch diagrams) if desired. Appliqué B to the center of the block. Trim the block to 9½ inches square.

HOW TO MAKE THIS QUILT

This quilt is designed to be a full-size quilt measuring 81×99 inches, including a 4½-inch-wide mitered inner border, and half-blocks used as the outer border with 4½-inch corner squares.

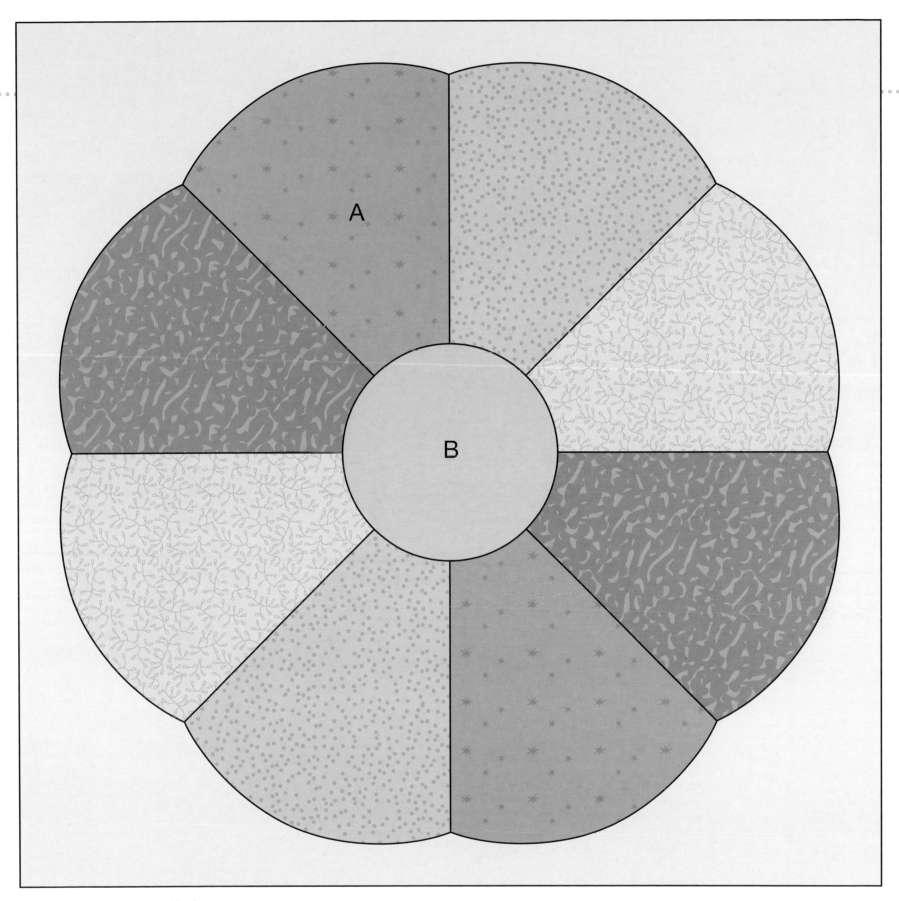

D<small>RESDEN</small> P<small>LATE</small> *full-size block*

butterfly

HOW TO CONSTRUCT THIS BLOCK

Fold a 9½-inch background square diagonally twice in an X; press. Appliqué A on the background square. Appliqué B over A. Using the stitch diagrams on page 214, embroider the wings and antennae using a stem stitch. Blanket-stitch around the wings to complete the block.

HOW TO MAKE THIS QUILT

This quilt is designed to be a twin-size quilt measuring 63×90 inches, including 4½-inch-wide sashing. The outer border is 13½ inches wide with mitered corners.

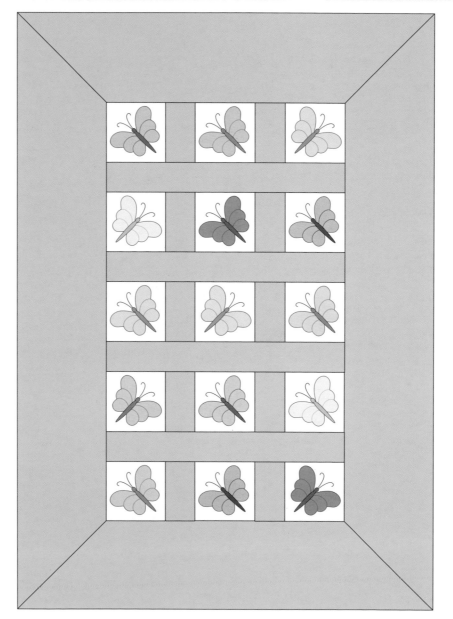

A

B

Butterfly *full-size block*

crazy ann

HOW TO CONSTRUCT THIS BLOCK

Sew light A to each short side of dark B (4 times). Sew dark A to each short side of light B (4 times). Sew light ABA to the bottom of dark ABA (4 times). Noting placement, stitch ABAABA to ABAABA (2 times). Sew the two units together to make a center unit. Sew a light B to two adjoining sides of C (4 times). Sew one BCB to opposite sides of the center unit. Sew one BCB to each of the remaining sides of the center unit.

HOW TO MAKE THIS QUILT

This quilt is designed to be a twin-size quilt measuring 72×94½ inches. The quilt has a pieced border with the same width as the sashing strips.

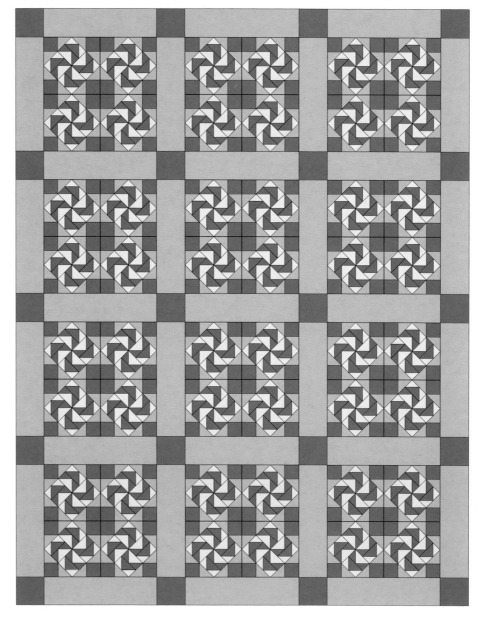

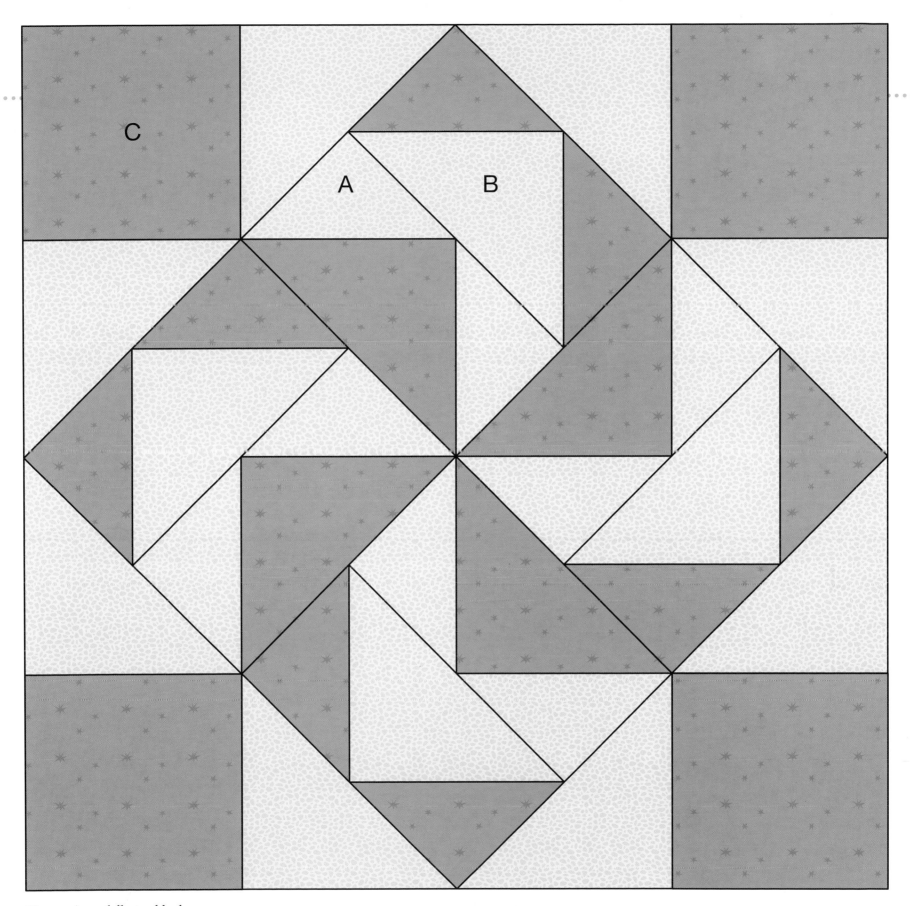

CRAZY ANN *full-size block*

pinwheel

HOW TO CONSTRUCT THIS BLOCK

Sew A piece to B piece to make a triangle (4 times). Sew AB to AB (2 times). Join the two units together.

HOW TO MAKE THIS QUILT

This quilt is designed to be a twin-size quilt measuring 75×84 inches. We have used a 1½-inch-wide solid color border with mitered corners as shown.

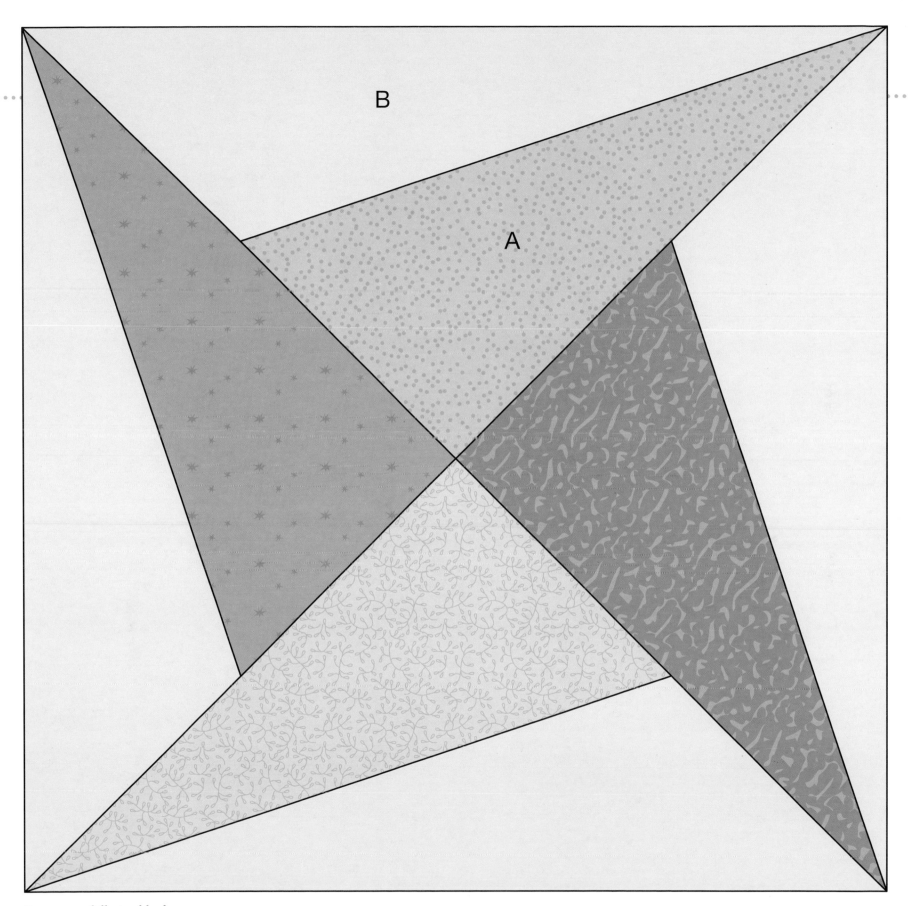

B

A

PINWHEEL *full-size block*

country decision

HOW TO CONSTRUCT THIS BLOCK

Lay out all pieces in correct position, watching placement carefully. Sew A to B (4 times). Sew AB to C (4 times). Sew C to C (4 times). Sew CC to F (4 times). Sew CCF to G (4 times). Sew two Cs to H (8 times). Sew CCFG to CCH (4 times) to make a Unit. Sew CCH to I (4 times). Sew CCHI to Unit (4 times). Sew a Unit to ABC (2 times); add a Unit (2 times). Sew ABC to F; add ABC. Sew ABCFABC to connect the Units.

HOW TO MAKE THIS QUILT

This quilt is designed to be a twin-size quilt measuring 64×91 inches. We have used 2-, 1-, and 2-inch-wide solid color borders to finish the quilt as shown.

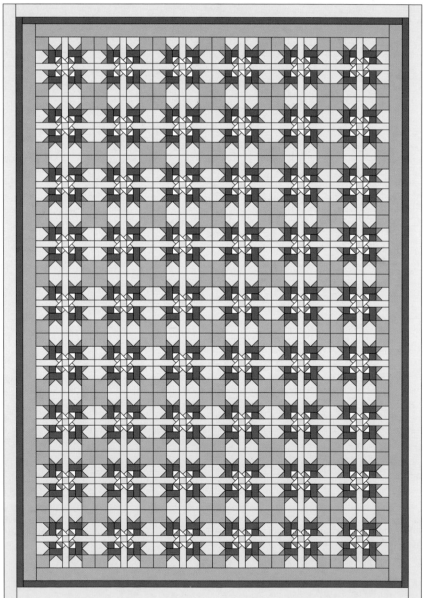

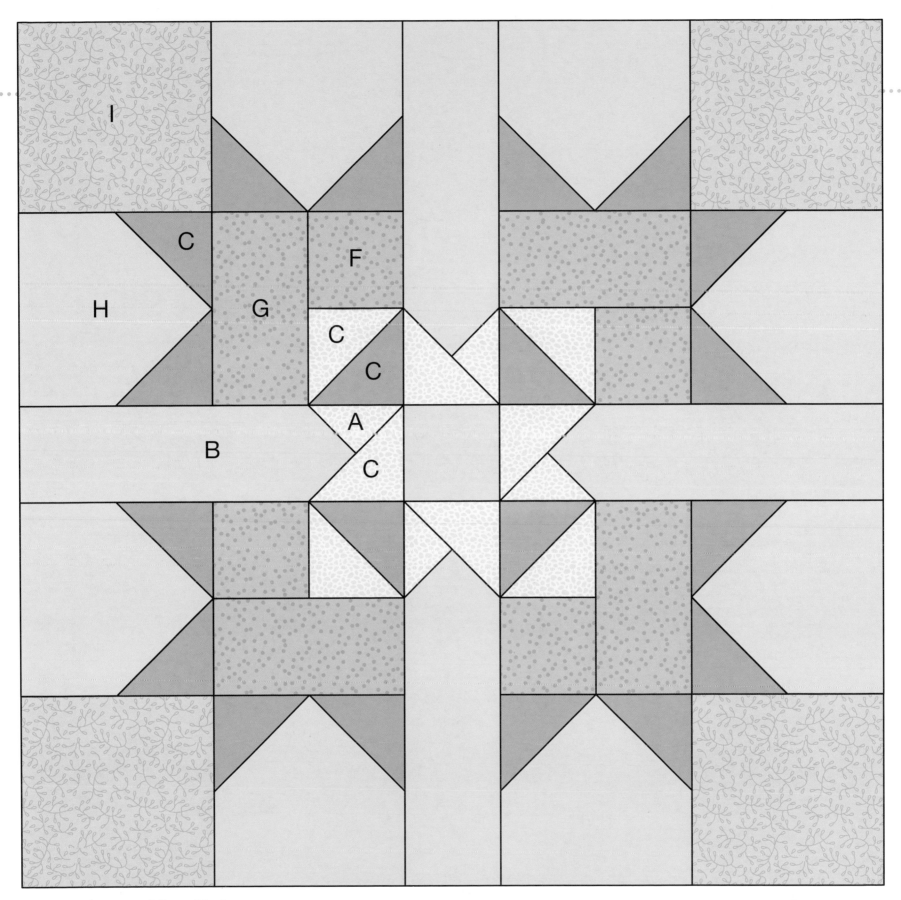

Country Decision *full-size block*

favorite geometrics

From the bold colors and shapes in an Amish Shadows quilt to the clever optics of a Card Tricks block, the basic geometric shapes of these classic patterns continue to offer stunning and vibrant quilts.

INSPIRATION

While many pieced quilts fall into the category of being geometric by nature, some blocks and finished quilts depend on straight and orderly lines to create the desired effect. The additional use of color within these shapes makes for stunning finished pieces.

Nowhere is the use of order and geometry better seen than in Amish quilts. Quilts made by Amish women in the late 1800s and the early 1900s were utilitarian, yet are brilliant examples of rich, vibrant color. The austere Amish women created quilts so visually dramatic that they are now hailed as great works of art.

When the Amish came to America, their separateness and simple ways gave them a unique approach to quiltmaking. Early Amish quilts were notable for their somber colors as well as the plain and geometric designs. The limited colors were due in part to the limited number of colorfast dyes available before 1880. In addition, the Amish rules that governed plainness of dress and lifestyle also applied to quilts.

On the prairie and the prosperous farms of Pennsylvania, change inevitably crept into Amish societies. By 1890, Amish women used the new fabrics available to them to create some of the most stunning, richly colored geometric quilts in history.

The straightforward yet stunning features of simple geometric shapes were favorites far beyond the Amish communities.

Women loved piecing quilts using color and simple shapes to create works of art, and geometric designs were among the best-loved. By simply changing the arrangement of color in a geometric design, the look and feel of the quilt became personal as well as a work of art.

Patterned glassware, popular in the 1800s and early 1900s, had many pressed-in designs. This unusual carnival glass tumbler has a quilted pattern.

Some of the timeless and geometric designs include Ocean Waves, Amish Bars, Amish Cross, Criss Cross, Geometric Butterfly, Amish Nine-Patch, Jacob's Ladder, Amish Stripe, and Irish Chain.

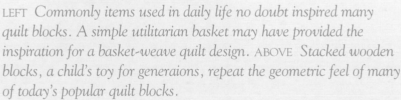

LEFT *Commonly items used in daily life no doubt inspired many quilt blocks. A simple utilitarian basket may have provided the inspiration for a basket-weave quilt design.* ABOVE *Stacked wooden blocks, a child's toy for generaions, repeat the geometric feel of many of today's popular quilt blocks.*

rectangle makes the square

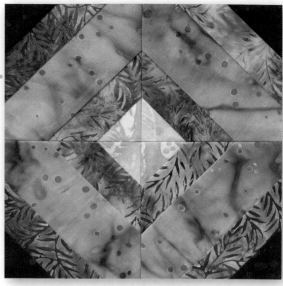

HOW TO CONSTRUCT THIS BLOCK

Sew A to B along long edge of A. Then join AB to C along long edge. Join second A and B, and sew to center C piece. Make four units. Join four units together to complete the block.

HOW TO MAKE THIS QUILT

This quilt is designed to be a twin-size quilt measuring 78×96 inches. It uses a 3-inch-wide solid color border as shown.

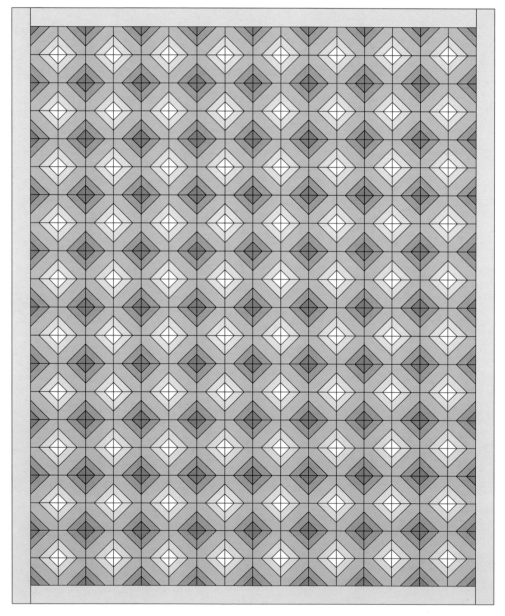

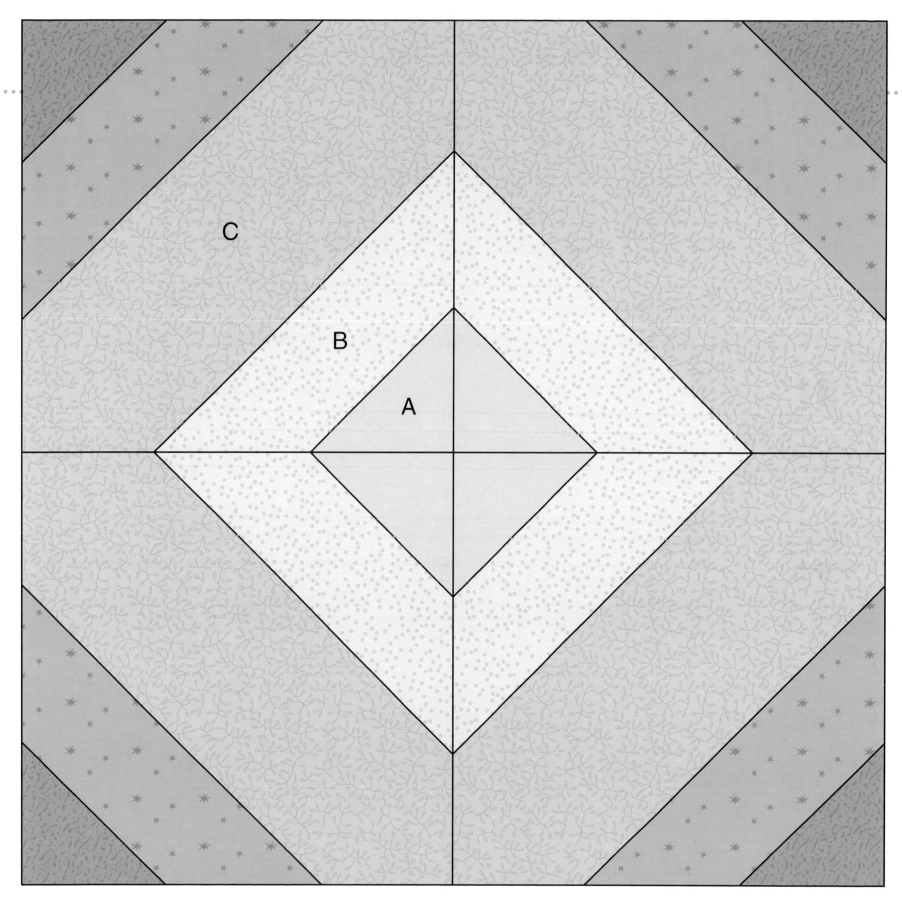

RECTANGLE MAKES THE SQUARE *full-size block*

color triangle

HOW TO CONSTRUCT THIS BLOCK

The pieces for this block could be constructed using a template, or you may cut a 3⅞-inch square in half diagonally to create two A triangles. Cut a total of 18 A triangles. Sew two A pieces together along long edges. Make a total of nine AA units. Join AA units together into three rows, then sew the three rows together to make block.

HOW TO MAKE THIS QUILT

This quilt is designed to be a full-size quilt measuring 81×99 inches. It uses the 4½-inch-wide Triangles border (see page 208), as shown.

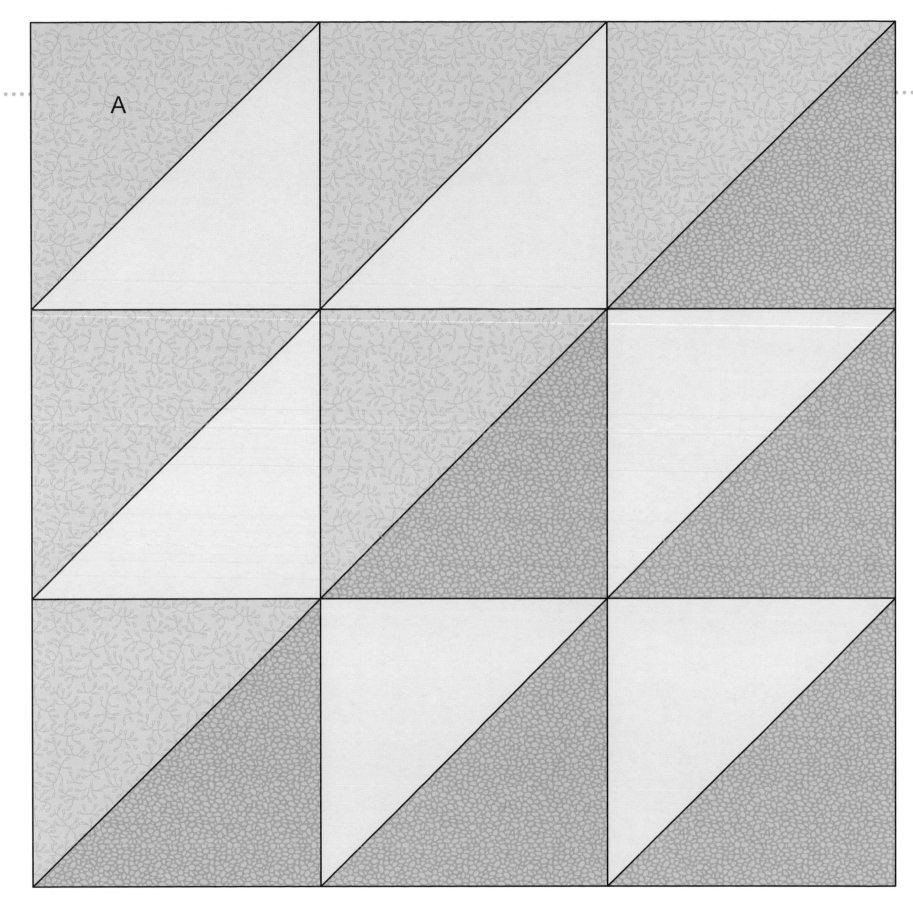

A

Color Triangle *full-size block*

amish cross

HOW TO CONSTRUCT THIS BLOCK

Make BB unit (8 times). Sew A piece to BB unit (4 times). Sew BB unit to A piece (4 times). Sew AB units to BA units (4 times) forming corner AB squares. Join two AB squares together with C piece in between (2 times) to form top and bottom rows. Sew two C pieces with D square in between for the center row. Sew top and center rows together; add bottom row.

HOW TO MAKE THIS QUILT

This quilt is designed to be a twin-size quilt measuring 63×90 inches. It uses a 4½-inch-wide solid color border and corner squares as shown.

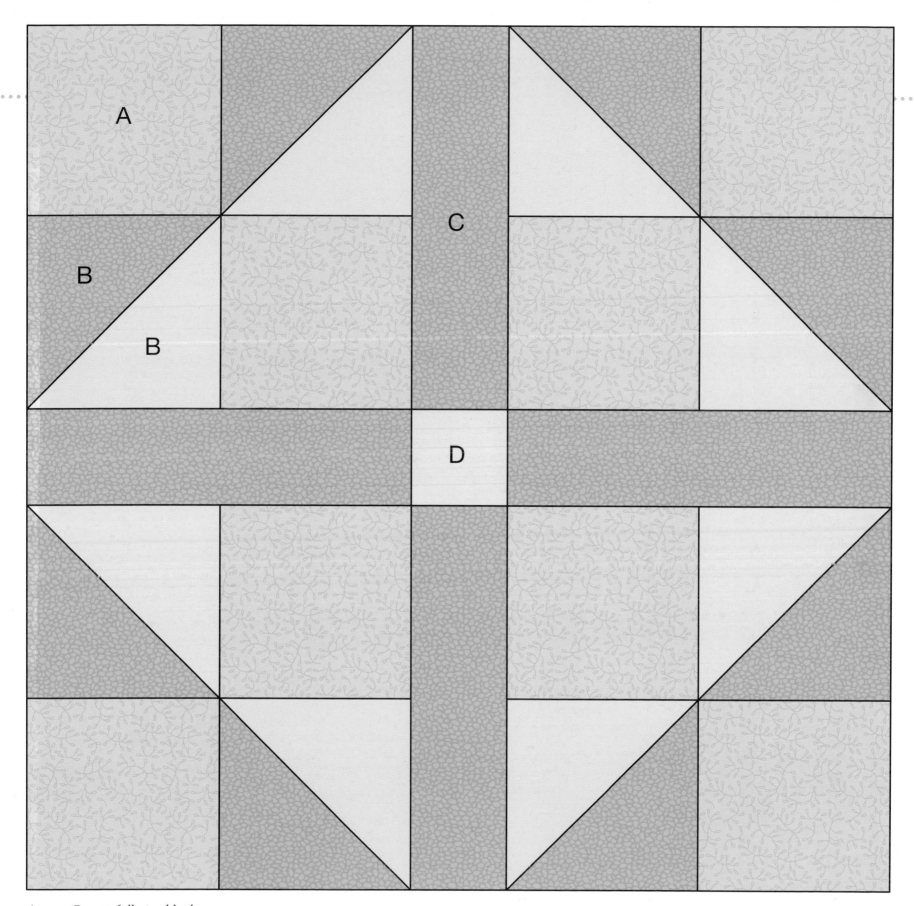

AMISH CROSS *full-size block*

middle ground

HOW TO CONSTRUCT THIS BLOCK

Join A, B, and Ar (four times). Join C section to each side of ABAr sections. Attach to center section D.

look again

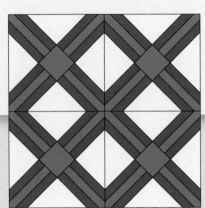

The pieced stripes that come together make a distinct and exciting pattern when the blocks are abutted in the finished quilt. The new squares that form between the blocks create a very optical look.

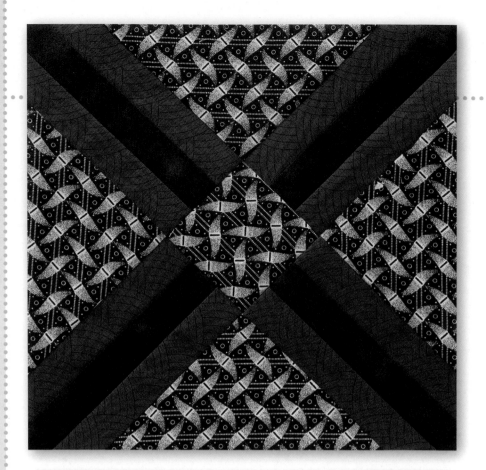

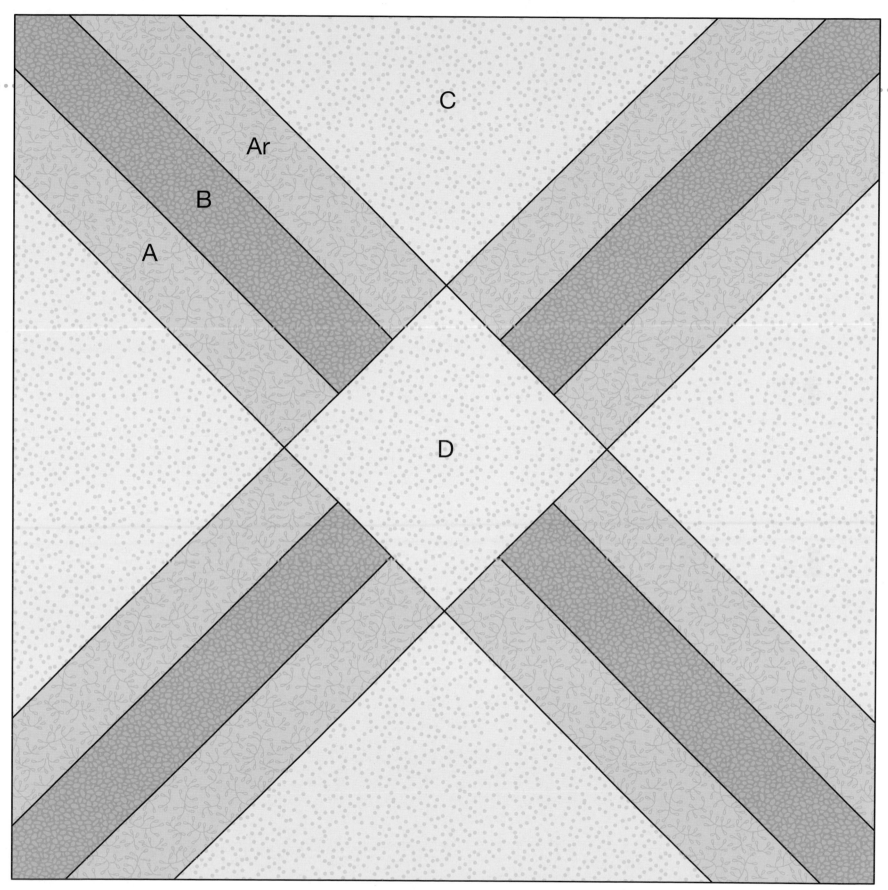

MIDDLE GROUND *full-size block*

country pinwheel

HOW TO CONSTRUCT THIS BLOCK

Use template or cut 3⅛-inch squares in half diagonally to create two A triangles. Cut a total of 16 dark A triangles and 16 light A triangles. Sew one light A to one dark A along long edges. Make a total of 16 AA units. Join the AA units together into two rows, then add the next two rows to make block.

HOW TO MAKE THIS QUILT

This quilt is designed to be a twin-size quilt measuring 66×93 inches. It uses a 1½-inch-wide solid color border with mitered corners as shown.

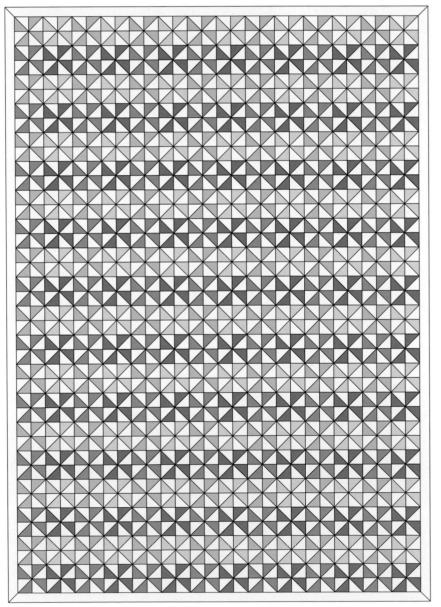

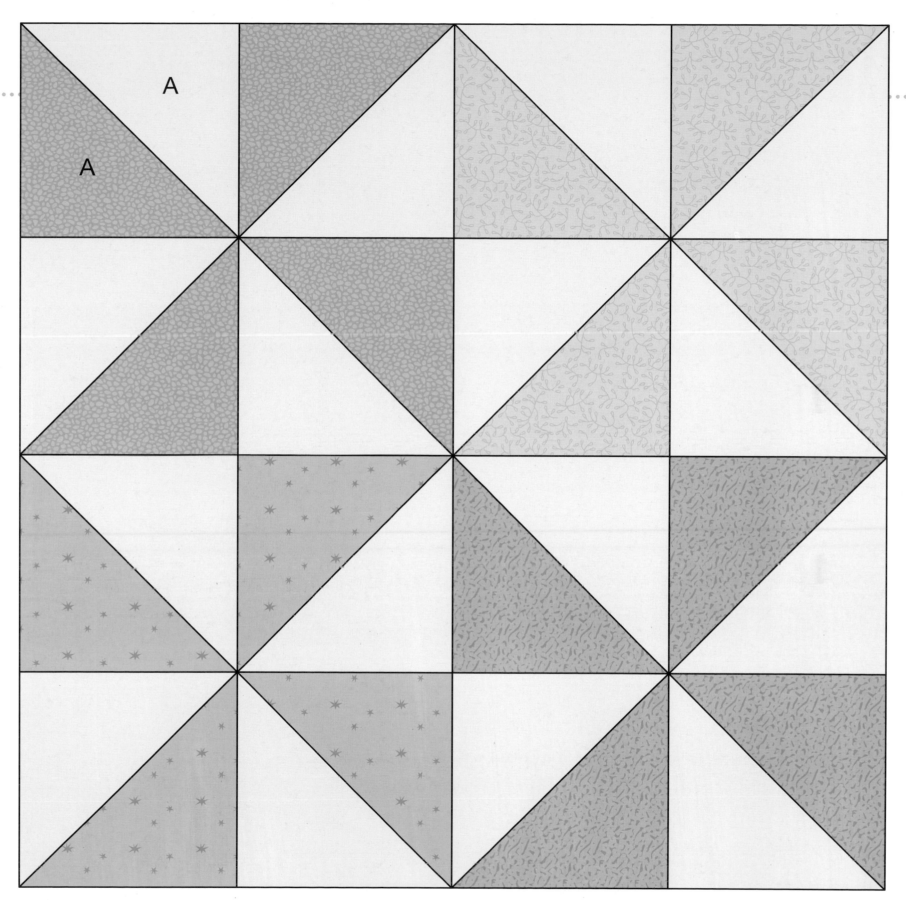

C OUNTRY P INWHEEL *full-size block*

geometric butterfly

HOW TO CONSTRUCT THIS BLOCK

This block is made in wo asymmetrical sections. Left section: Sew B to C; 1 to A; D to E. Join these units and add H. Right section: Sew Ar to Ir: Dr to Er; F to G. Join these units and add Hr. Sew the two sections together to complete the block.

about this block

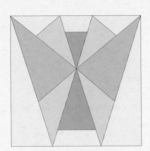

The butterfly motif has long been a favorite among quilters, offering the opportunity to show off glorious colors of fabric in prints that are suitable for this natural wonder. The amazing geometric proportion of the butterfly lends itself to a wonderful pieced work of art.

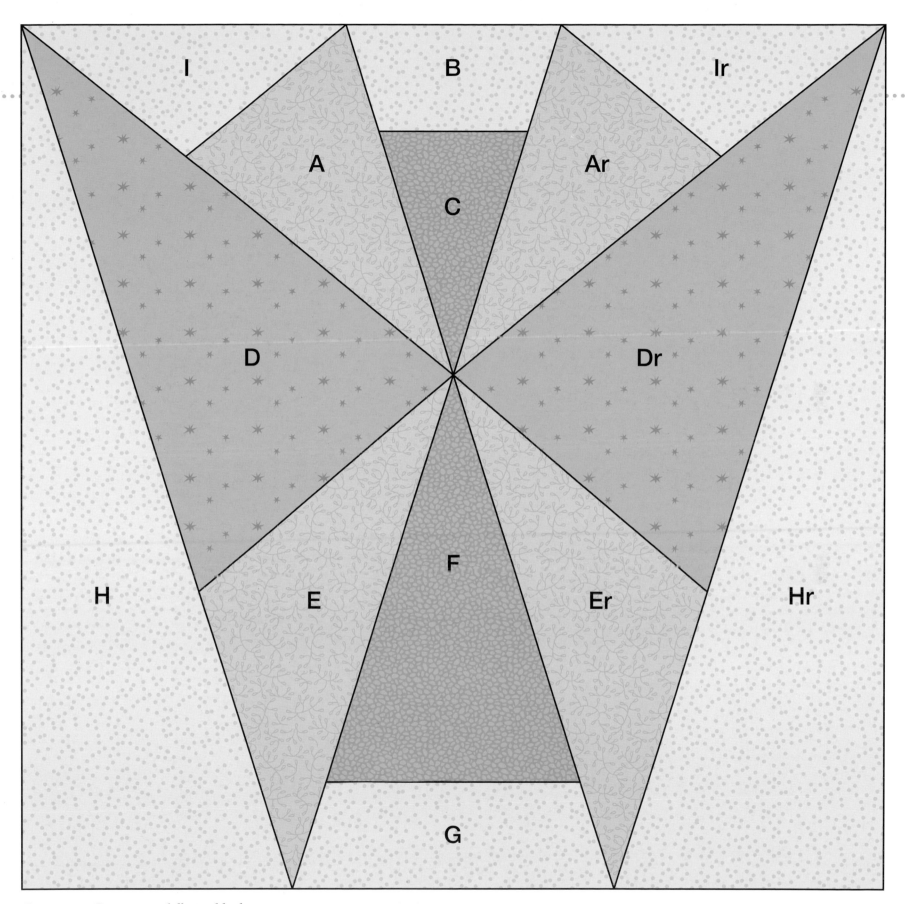

GEOMETRIC BUTTERFLY *full-size block*

woven ribbon

HOW TO CONSTRUCT
THIS BLOCK

Sew one B to side of one D (4 times).
Sew BD to C (4 times). Add B to other
side of CBD unit (4 times). Sew E to
BCBD (4 times). Sew F to BCBDE
(4 times). Sew G to FBCBDE (4 times).
Sew H to each side of two units. These
will become two opposite corner units.
(The remaining two units will become
the end units of the center square.)
Sew four J pieces around center square
A, setting in corners where necessary;
add end units to opposite sides of
center square. Sew one corner unit to
center unit; add remaining corner unit
to oppostite side of center unit to
complete the block.

HOW TO MAKE
THIS QUILT

This quilt is designed to be twin-size
quilt measuring 66x93 inches. It uses a
1½-inch-wide solid color border with
mitered corners as shown.

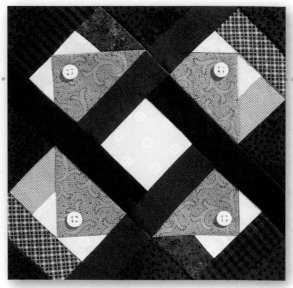

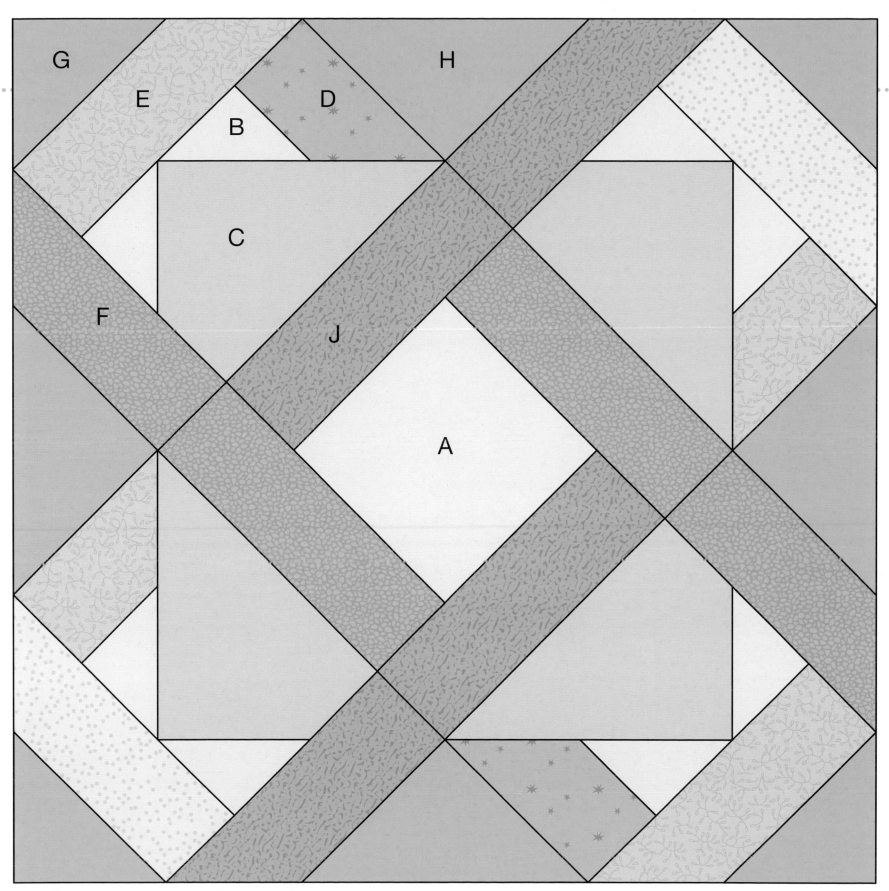

WOVEN RIBBON *full-size block*

jewel star

HOW TO CONSTRUCT THIS BLOCK

Sew A to B (2 times). Sew AB unit to C (2 times). Sew Ar to Br (2 times). Sew ArBr to C (2 times). Sew ABCBrAr unit to D (2 times). Join the two halves to complete the block.

HOW TO MAKE THIS QUILT

This quilt is designed to be a queen-size quilt measuring 90x90 inches. It uses three 2¼-inch-wide solid color borders and a 4½-inch Triangles border, (see page 208) as shown.

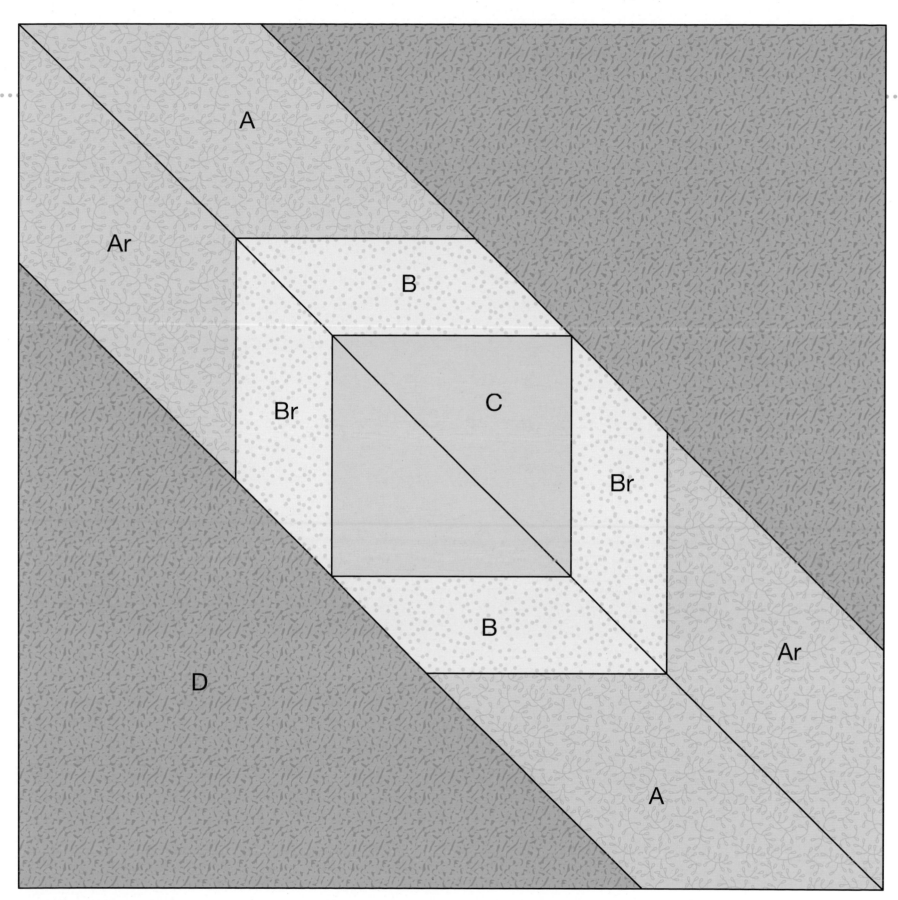

A

Ar

B

Br

C

Br

B

Ar

D

A

JEWEL STAR *full-size block*

king's crown

HOW TO CONSTRUCT THIS BLOCK

Make BCB unit (4 times); attach 2 of these units to opposite sides of D piece. Add A pieces at each end of BCB unit (2 times). Sew ABCBA units to each side of center unit to make the block.

about this block

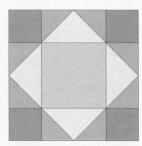

Actually known as King David's Crown by some quilters, this quilt block is a classic with many stitching possibilities. Because the center of the block is a simple square, the space can be used to feature a special conversation print or as a signature block. Signature blocks, blocks where the stitcher and her friends signed their names, were popular in the 1920s and 1930s.

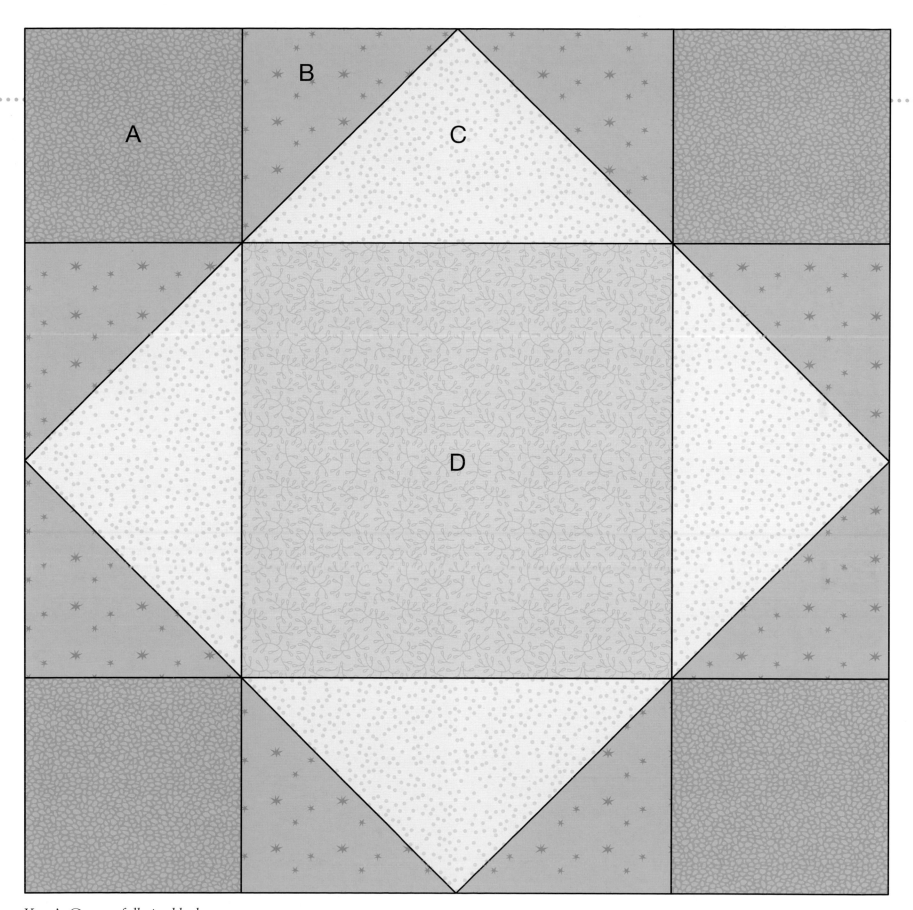

A

B

C

D

KING'S CROWN *full-size block*

turkey tracks variation

HOW TO CONSTRUCT THIS BLOCK

Make four Unit 1 corner sections by joining unit in alphabetical order. Make 2 rows by joining Unit 1 sections with an I square in the middle. Make the center AB section. Join I squares to opposite sides of the AB section. Join the rows together.

look again

By abutting these blocks side by side, a new block is created in each set of four that is joined. Varying the lights and darks of the fabrics will yield different looks within the finished piece.

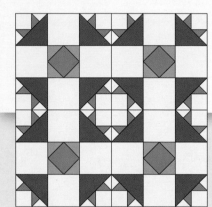

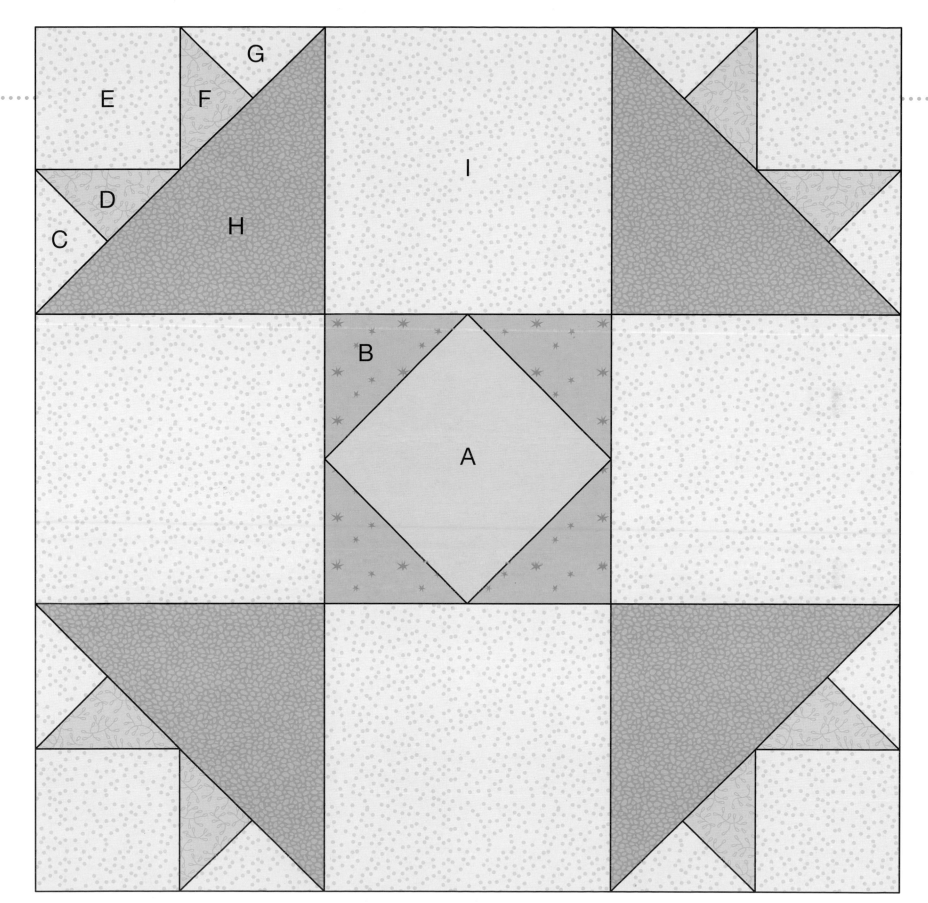

TURKEY TRACKS VARIATION *full-size block*

hugs and kisses

HOW TO CONSTRUCT THIS BLOCK

Sew A pieces together to make Nine-Patch center. Sew BB unit (4 times). Sew the A pieces together to make four-patch (4 times). Sew two A Four-Patch units together with BB unit in between (2 times). Sew two BB units together with A Nine-Patch in between. Sew two ABA rows together with BAB row in between. Sew C piece to two opposite sides of assembled AB block. Sew ACA unit (2 times). Sew ACA strips to top and bottom of pieced ABC block.

Note: Depending on color arrangement, the block will appear to resemble either an "O" or "X" motif—thus a hug or a kiss.

HOW TO MAKE THIS QUILT

This quilt is designed to be a full-size quilt measuring 81×99 inches. It uses two 4½-inch-wide solid color borders and Four-Patch corners as shown.

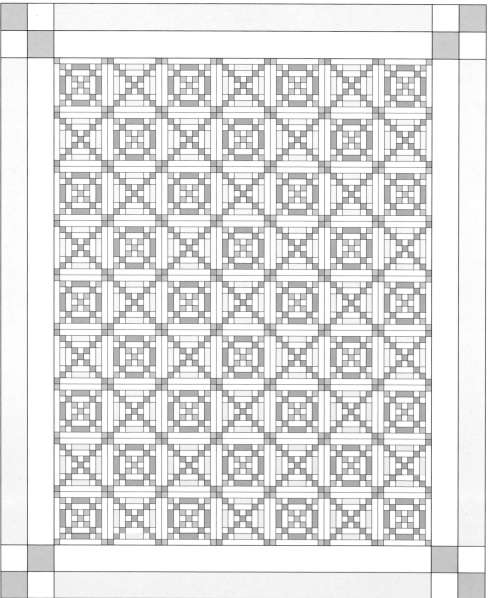

HUGS AND KISSES *full-size block*

amish shadows

HOW TO CONSTRUCT THIS BLOCK

This block can be made by sewing 9 units together. Each unit is made by sewing A to B, then to C, and then to D—then combining the 9 units into the block. But it is easier to sew three strips together, then cut out 9 squares by laying a square template on the sewn strip. Once you have the 9 squares assembled, join them into rows, then join the rows to make the block.

look again

By *turning each block a quarter turn (in each set of four), a new graphic look is created with a plain square* in the middle of the blocks. This design will be accomplished no matter where the lights and darks are placed on the block.

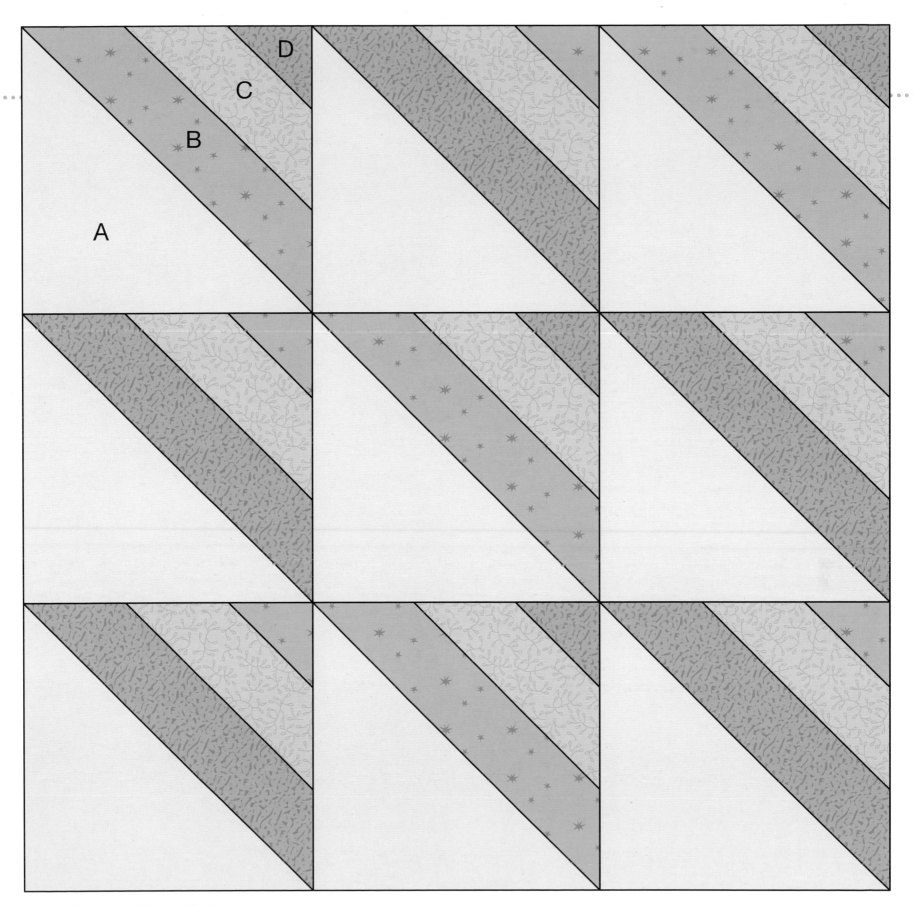

Amish Shadows *full-size block*

streak of lightning

HOW TO CONSTRUCT THIS BLOCK

Make AA unit (16 times). Join the units in rows, then join the rows to make the block.

about this block

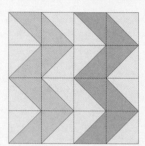

This block works best when definite light and dark fabrics are chosen. The square is cut diagonally, forming a triangle yielding an arrangement of light and that creates the zigzag effect. "Streak of Lightning" is also known as "ZigZag." Try using lights and darks in unusual patterns such as the bandanas as shown above.

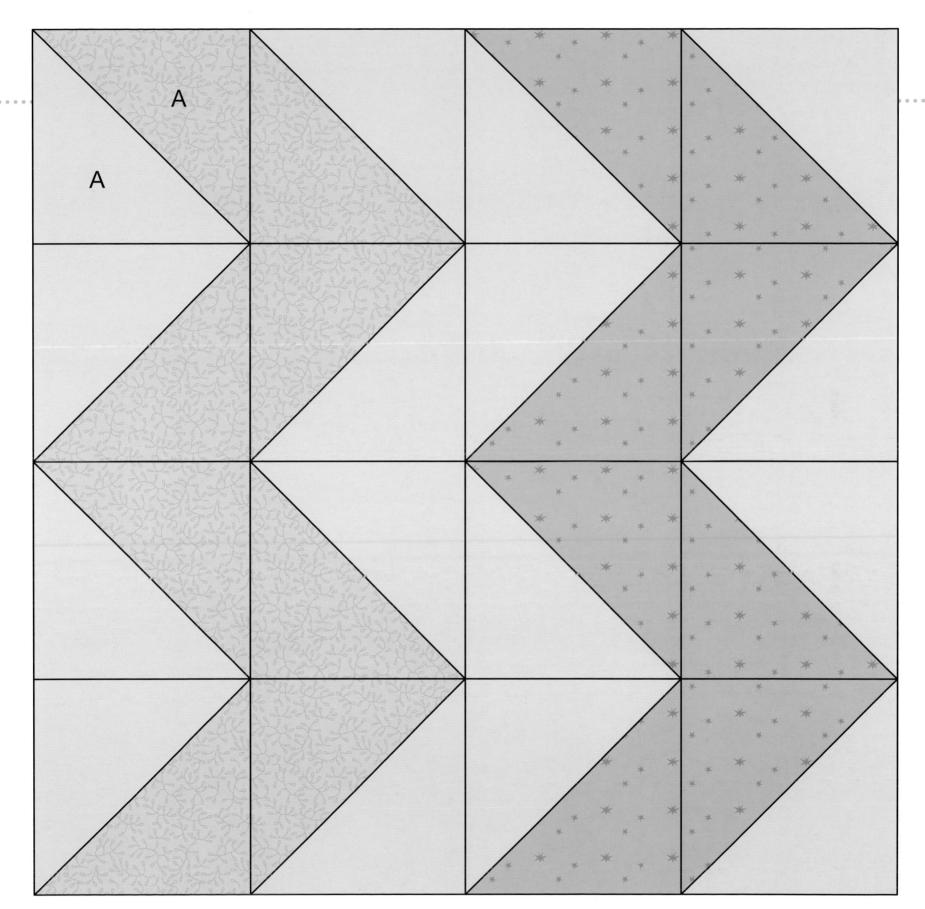

STREAK OF LIGHTNING *full-size block*

geometry

HOW TO CONSTRUCT THIS BLOCK

Join A and Ar; add B (4 times). Join the AArB units into pairs, then sew together along the diagonal to complete the block.

about this block

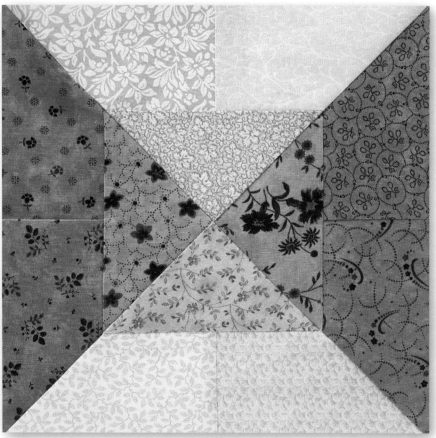

Color plays a key role in every pieced or appliquéd block, but if the block is very geometric. color can be the ingredient that makes the quilt exquisite.

Use shades and tints of color from one color family for a stunning look and plan the finished quilt on a grid before choosing and placing the colors.

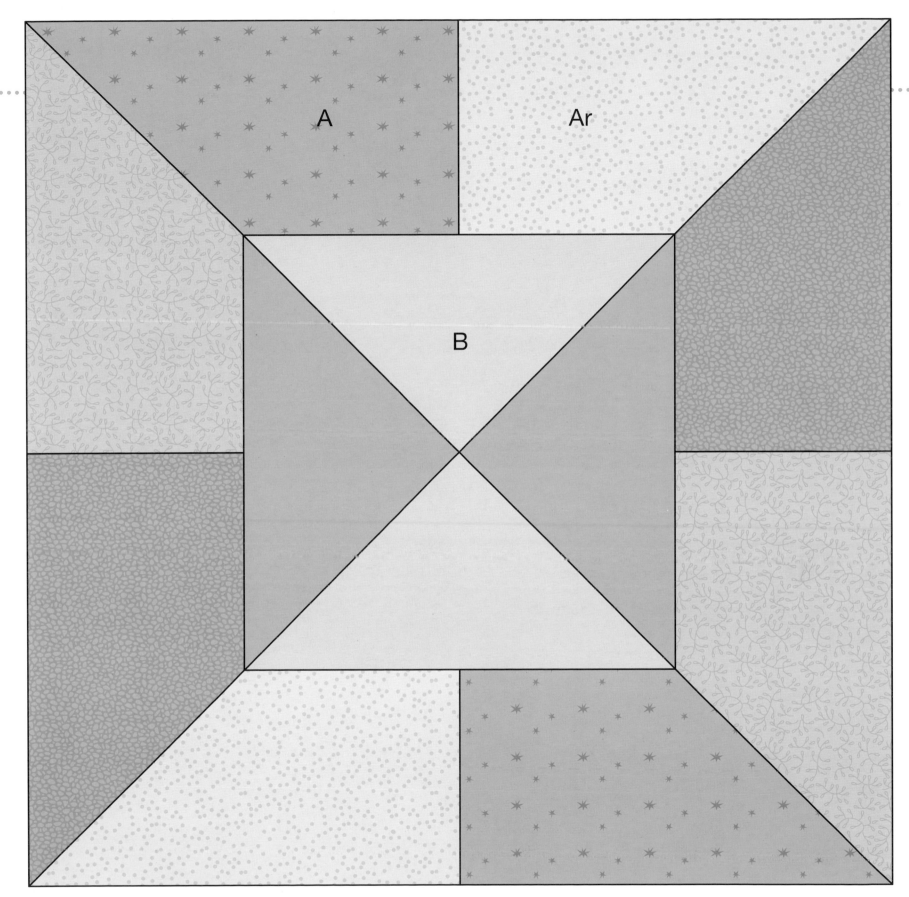

A

Ar

B

G<small>EOMETRY</small> *full-size block*

waves

HOW TO CONSTRUCT THIS BLOCK

Make A section by joining pieces A and B. Repeat to make a total of 16 A sections. Join as shown in 4 rows of 4 squares. Join the rows to complete the block.

look again

This very geometric and traditional block creates the feeling of waves or movement when the blocks are placed side by side.

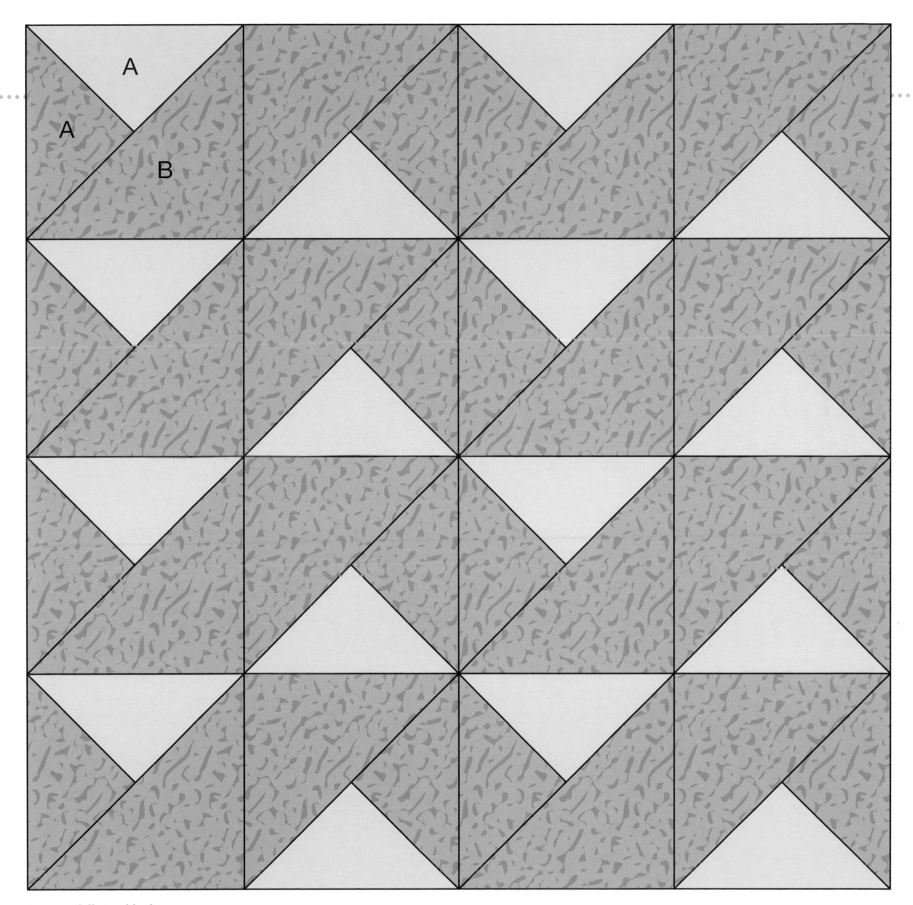

WAVES *full-size block*

card tricks

HOW TO CONSTRUCT THIS BLOCK

Make AA units (4 times). Make BBBB unit. Make ABB unit (4 times). Make rows AA/ABB/AA, ABB/BBBB/ABB, AA/ABB/AA. Join rows to make the block.

look again

An optical illusion is created that is very three-dimensional when these blocks are each rotated before piecing them in groups of four.

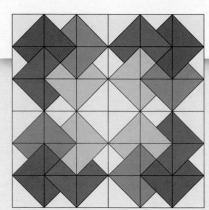

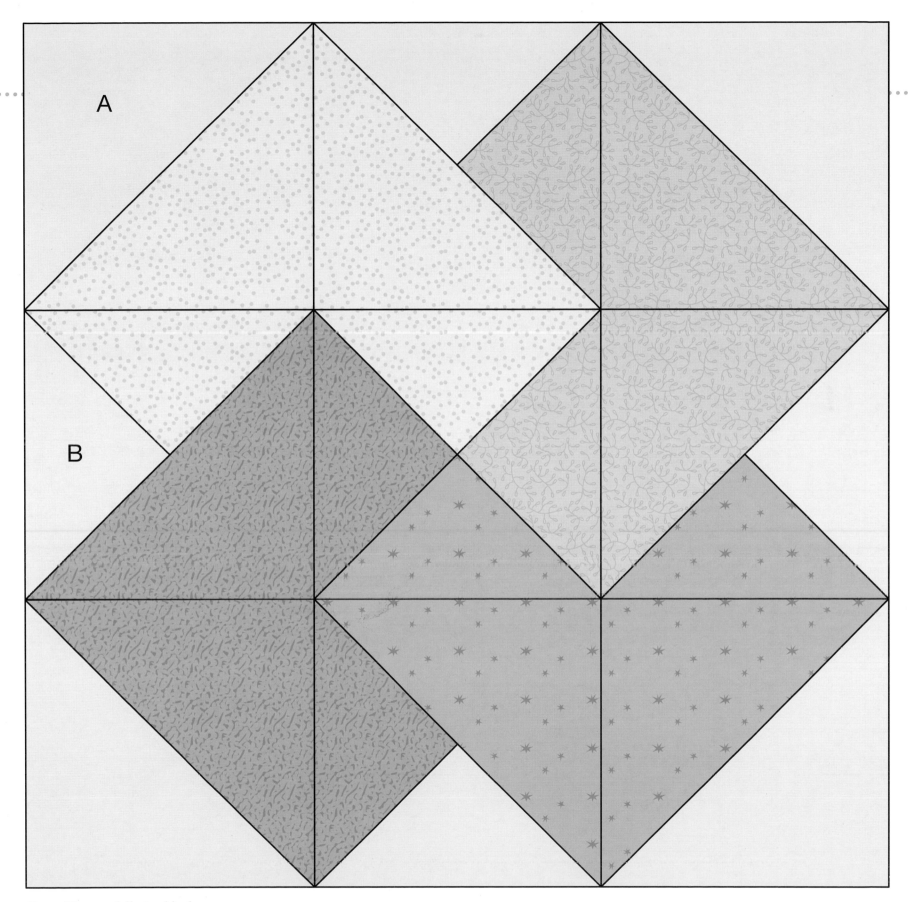

A

B

Card Tricks *full-size block*

criss cross

HOW TO CONSTRUCT THIS BLOCK

Sew light A to dark A (2 times). Add light A (2 times). Sew AAA to each long side of B to make a center ABA. Sew C to opposite sides of A (4 times). Sew CAC to B (4 times). Sew CACB to opposite sides of center ABA. Sew C to opposite sides of CACB (2 times). Sew CACCBC to opposite sides of the center unit. Sew D to each corner of the block.

HOW TO MAKE THIS QUILT

This quilt is designed to be a king-size quilt measuring 117×117 inches. Five blocks are set with four 9-inch setting squares to make a 27-inch unit. Five units alternate with 27-inch setting squares. The inner border is 9 inches wide, and the outer border is made up of quilt blocks.

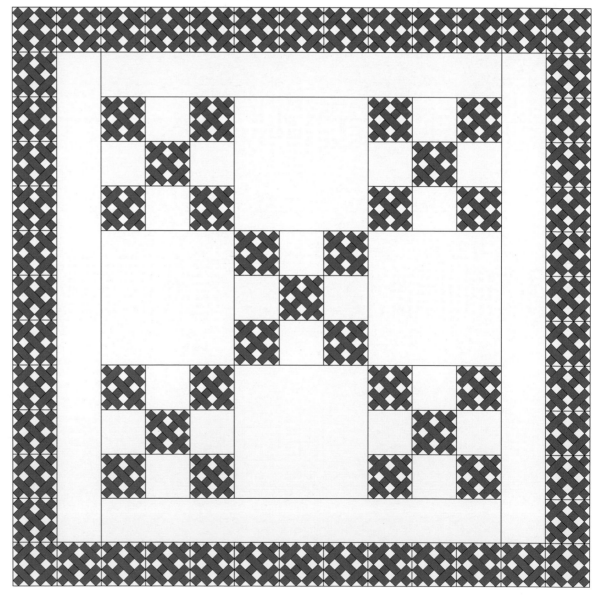

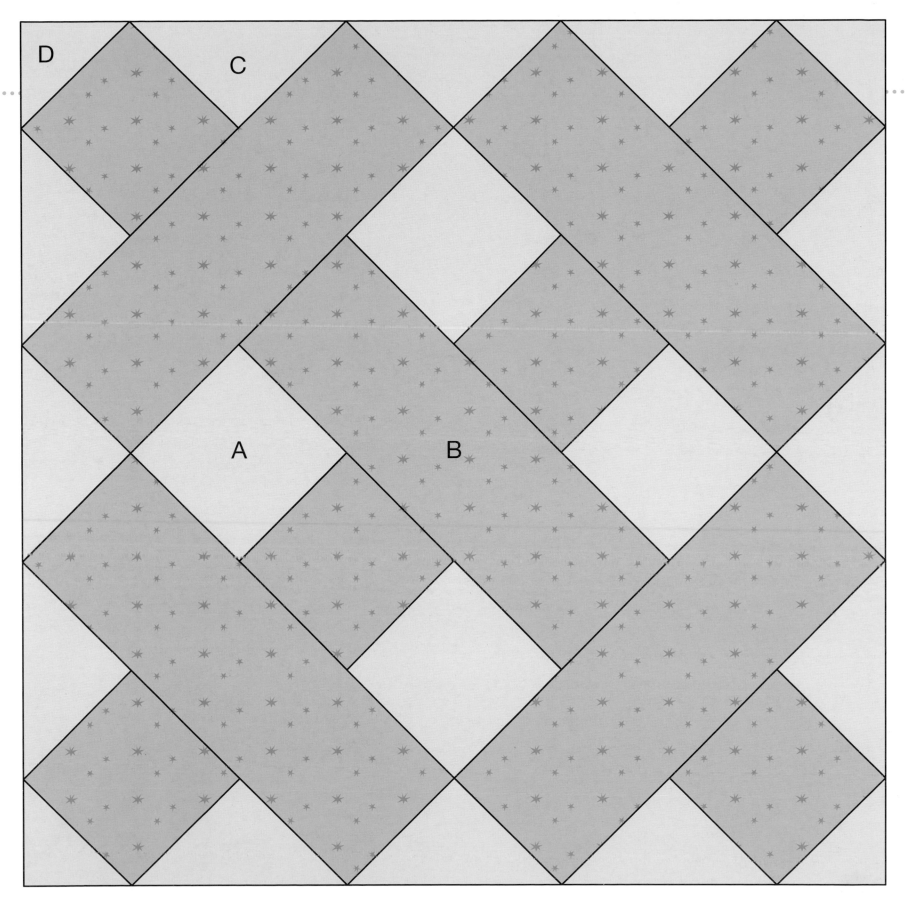

D
C
A
B

Criss Cross *full-size block*

delectable mountains

HOW TO CONSTRUCT THIS BLOCK

Sew A to A (6 times). Sew three AA units together (2 times). Sew one AAA unit to the left side of C. Sew B to the remaining AAA unit. Stitch BAAA to the bottom of AC. Add A to AAA (2 times). Sew D to ABC.

HOW TO MAKE THIS QUILT

This quilt is designed to be a queen-size quilt measuring 93½×111½ inches, with the blocks arranged into pinwheels. The 1¾-inch-wide inner border is made up of alternating triangle-squares. The 9-inch-wide outer border is mitered.

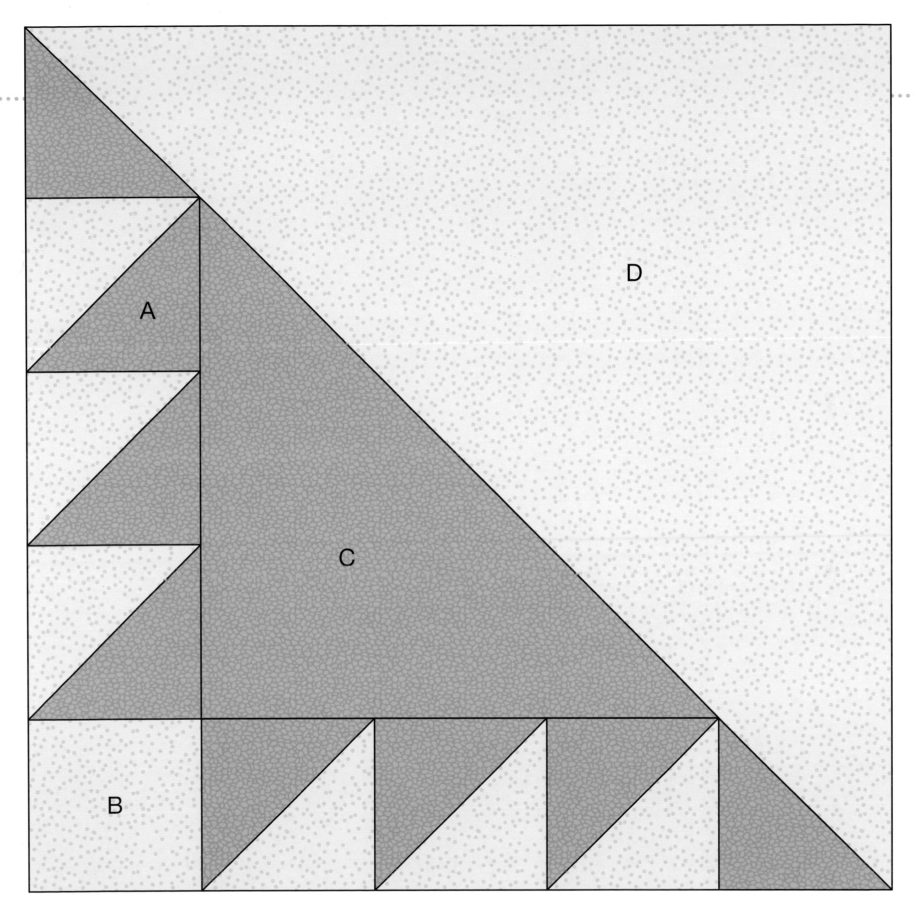

Delectable Mountains *full-size block*

colorado block

HOW TO CONSTRUCT THIS BLOCK

Sew light A to dark A (8 times). Sew dark A to each short side of B (4 times). Center Unit: Sew AA to AA (2 times). Stitch AAAA to AAAA to make center block. Sew AA to ABA, and AA (2 times) to make Rows 1 and 3. Sew ABA to the left side of center block; add ABA to the right side of center block to make Row 2. Sew Row 1 to Row 2; add Row 3.

HOW TO MAKE THIS QUILT

This quilt is designed to be a queen-size quilt measuring 99×99 inches. White with light blue is used for the center block. Surrounding blocks are gradually darker, with the dark from the previous row becoming the light shade. The edge of the finished quilt is the edge of the block.

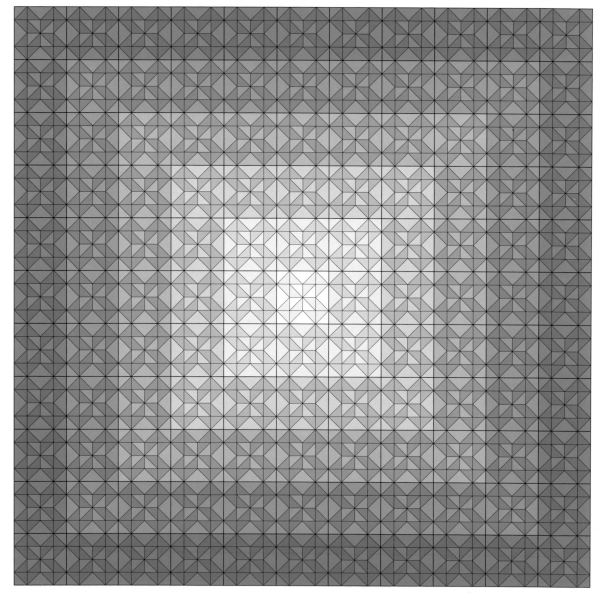

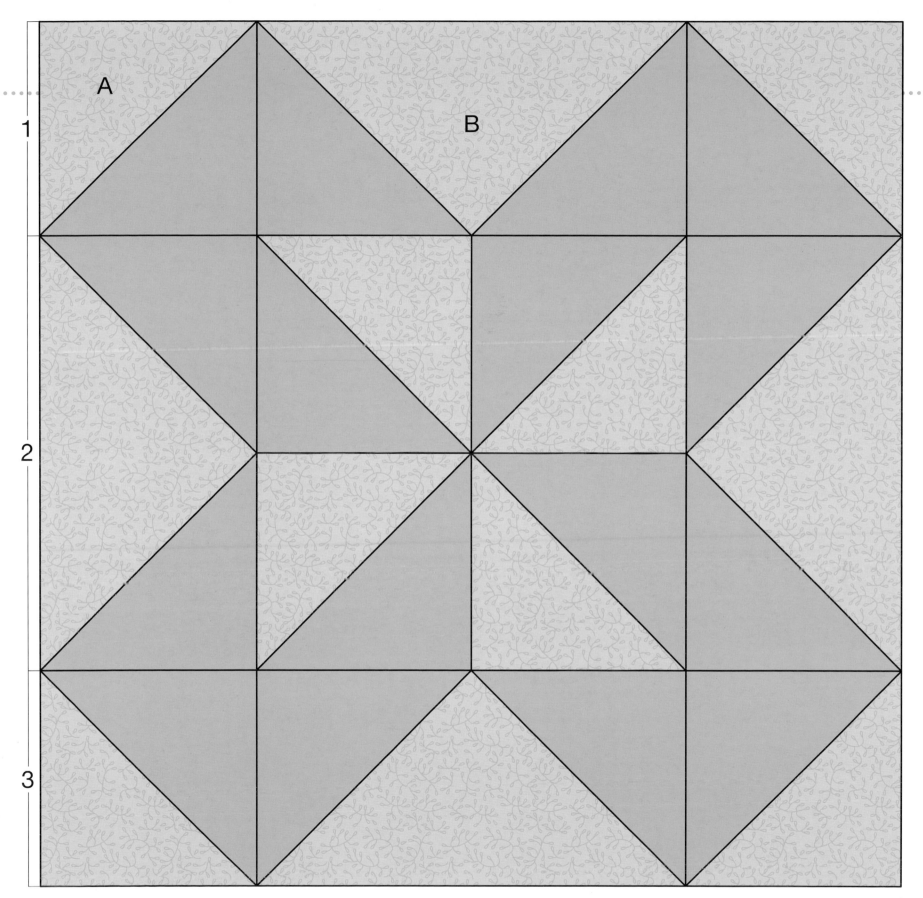

1

2

3

A

B

Colorado Block *full-size block*

sawtooth

HOW TO CONSTRUCT
THIS BLOCK

Sew B to B to make the center square.
Sew A to A (20 times). Sew four A
squares together (2 times). Stitch one
unit to the left side of the B square and
one unit to the right side of the B
square, noting color direction. Sew six
A squares together (2 times). Stitch
one unit to the top and one to the
bottom of the AB unit.

HOW TO MAKE
THIS QUILT

This quilt is designed to be a twin-size
quilt measuring 72×90 inches. The
edge of the finished quilt is the edge
of the block.

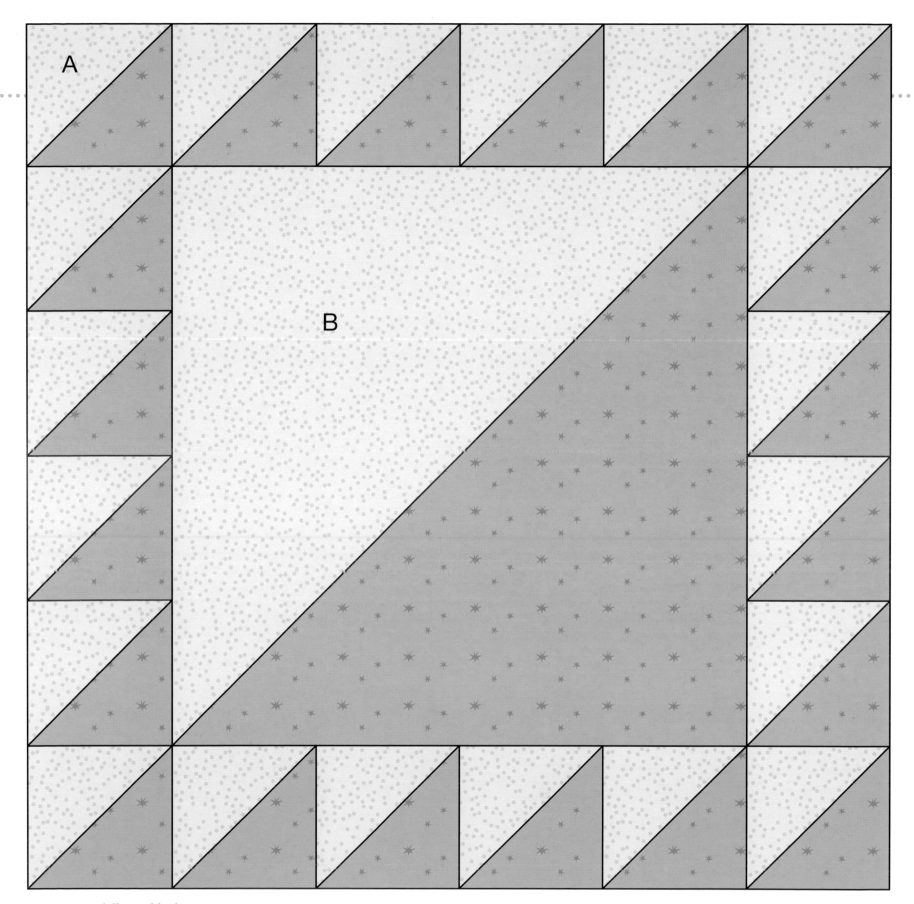

SAWTOOTH *full-size block*

irish chain

HOW TO CONSTRUCT THIS BLOCK

Repeat the following directions four times to complete five Nine-Patch blocks. Sew dark A to light A (3 times). To AA, sew a dark A (2 times) for the top and bottom rows. To AA, sew a light A for middle row. Join the three rows to complete one Nine-patch. Sew a Nine-Patch block to opposite sides of B (2 times) for Rows 1 and 3. Sew B to opposite sides of a Nine-Patch block for Row 2. Join the rows to complete one block.

HOW TO MAKE THIS QUILT

This quilt is designed to be a twin-size quilt measuring 72×90 inches with the edge of the block serving as the edge of the finished quilt.

IRISH CHAIN *full-size block*

borders & edgings

diamond & stripes

HOW TO CONSTRUCT THIS BORDER

Sew A and B together. Turn C on point. To the lower left edge, sew AB. To the opposite upper right edge, sew BA. The border is joined by sewing the ABCBA units diagonally to each other. For the corner unit, sew D and B together. Sew Dr and B together. Sew DBDrB together. To the B edges, add C. Sew the border strips to the quilt edge, stopping and starting ¼ inch from each end of the quilt top. Miter the border strips. Note: Pattern C measures 3 inches diagonally.

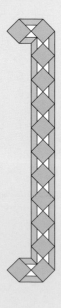

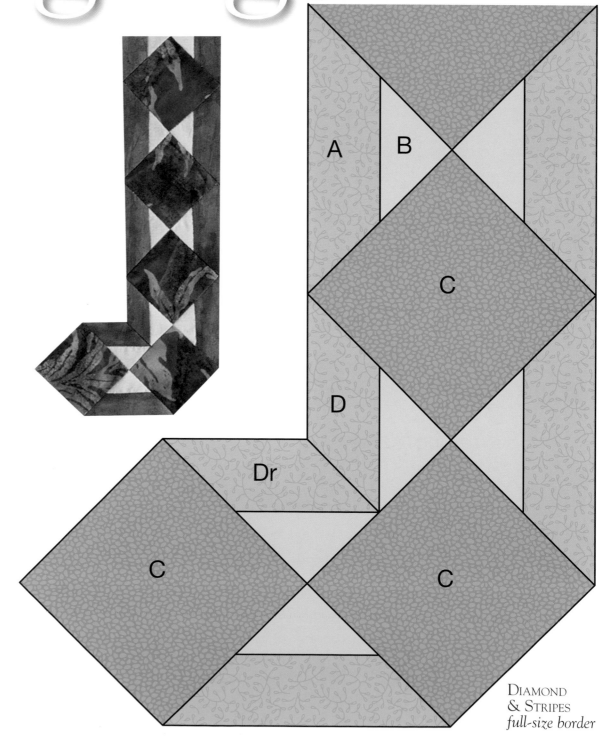

DIAMOND
& STRIPES
full-size border

eclectic

HOW TO CONSTRUCT THIS BORDER

This border is 4 inches wide and has a 6-inch repeat. Sew F border strip to each side of the quilt top; miter corners. Sew B to opposite sides of A (2 times). Sew B to remaining sides of A (2 times). Sew B to C (2 times). Sew BCB to BCB. Sew the required number of units together, referring to diagram, far left, for placement, to make four border strips. Sew D to each end of two border strips. Sew one border to the top and one to the bottom of the quilt top. Press the seams toward the outside border strip. Sew E to D (4 times). Press the seam toward D. Sew DE to each end of the two remaining border strips. Sew one DE border to each side of quilt top to complete border and quilt top.

ECLECTIC *full-size border*

triangles

HOW TO CONSTRUCT THIS BORDER

This border is 4½ inches wide and has a 4½-inch repeat. Sew B pieces to quilt edge, mitering the corners. (See page 215 for directions for mitering.) The B pieces should be cut in one continuous length to match each outside edge of the quilt. Sew A pieces together to complete desired length of quilt. Sew the AA strip to the outside edges of B. Sew C, the corner triangle, on each corner.

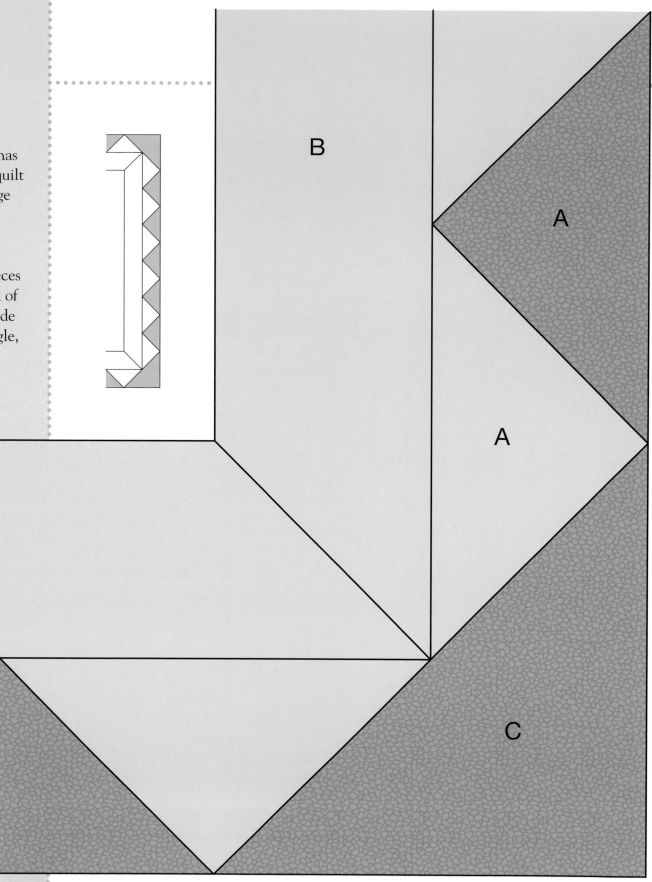

TRIANGLES *full-size border*

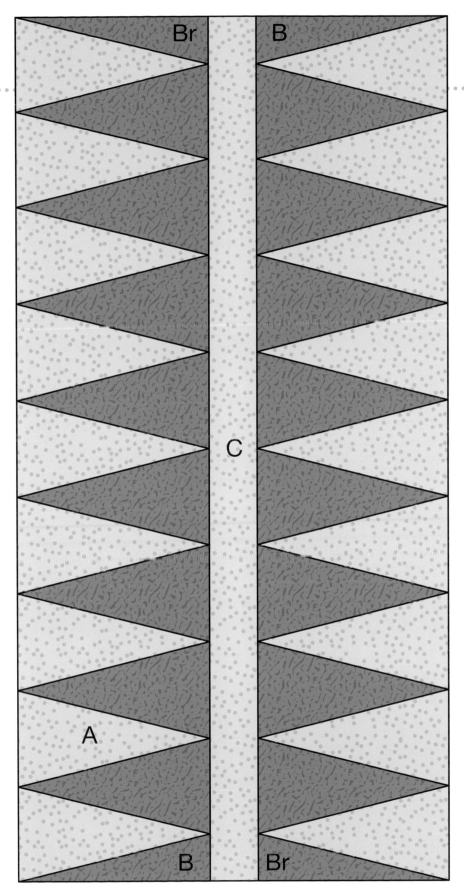

SAWTOOTH *full-size border*

sawtooth

HOW TO CONSTRUCT THIS BORDER

Sew light A to dark A (16 times). Sew AA to AA (8 times). Sew AAAA to AAAA (4 times). Sew 2 AAAAAAAA units together to make each side. Position the units to mirror each other. Sew B to the left side of each unit. Sew A to the left side of Br (2 times). Sew ABr to the right side of each unit. Follow the pattern diagram, left, to reverse positions of the units to mirror each other. Sew the dark bottom side of each unit to the long side of C, being careful to match up points on the opposite side.

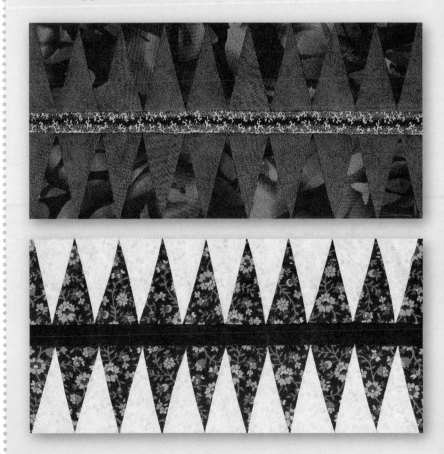

fan border

HOW TO CONSTRUCT THIS BORDER

Sew E to the top, bottom, and each side of the quilt top. Sew three As together. Appliqué B on the inside curve of AAA unit. Sew C on each side of AAAB unit. The completed border strip should begin and end with C. To make the corner block, sew six As together. Appliqué D on the inside curve. Sew to the corner diagonal edge.

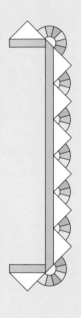

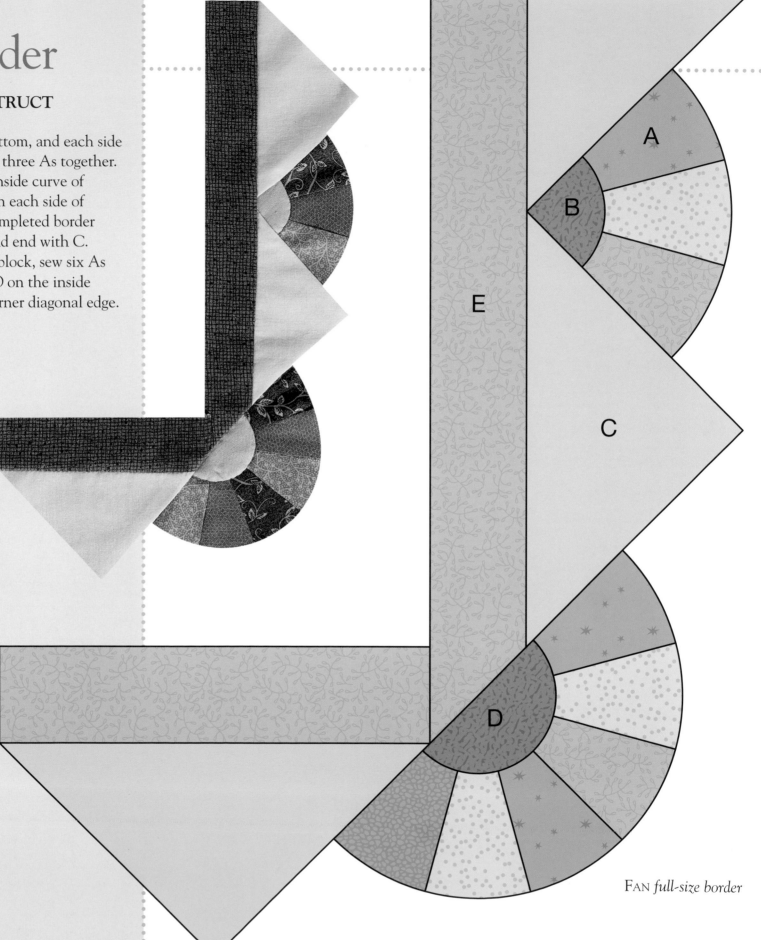

FAN full-size border

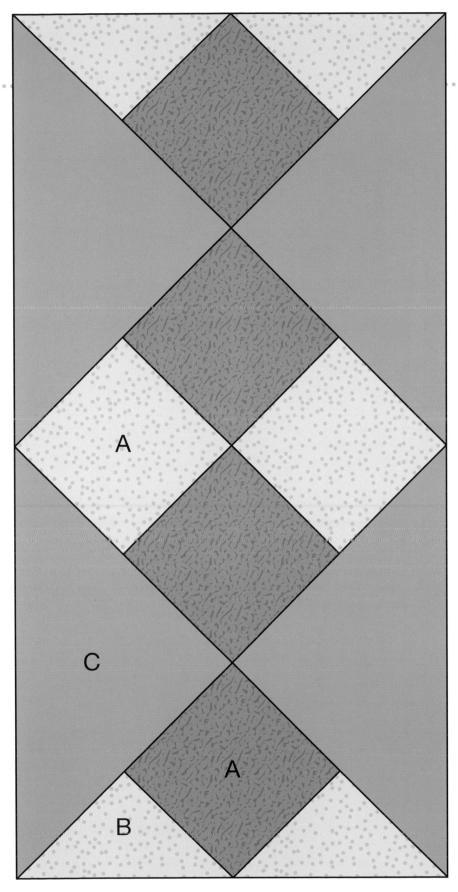

DIAMOND LINK *full-size border*

diamond link

HOW TO CONSTRUCT THIS BORDER

Sew light A to dark A (2 times). Reversing color placement, sew AA to AA. To opposite sides of AAAA, sew C. Sew light B to A (2 times); add B to the adjoining side (2 times). Sew C to ABB (2 times). Sew BABC to CAAAAC; add BABC to the opposite side.

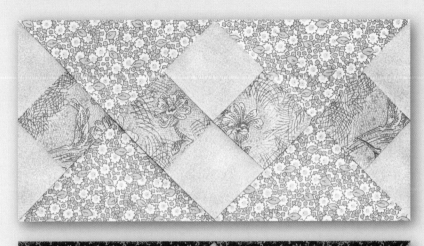

diamond edge

HOW TO CONSTRUCT THIS BORDER

This border is 5 inches wide and has a 6-inch repeat. Sew A to B in multiples for the length of the border. Sew the AB units together. At the end of the border strips, add a corner block C/Cr. Sew on the D strip. Sew the border units onto quilt edge, matching edges and seams of pieces C/Cr and D at the corners.

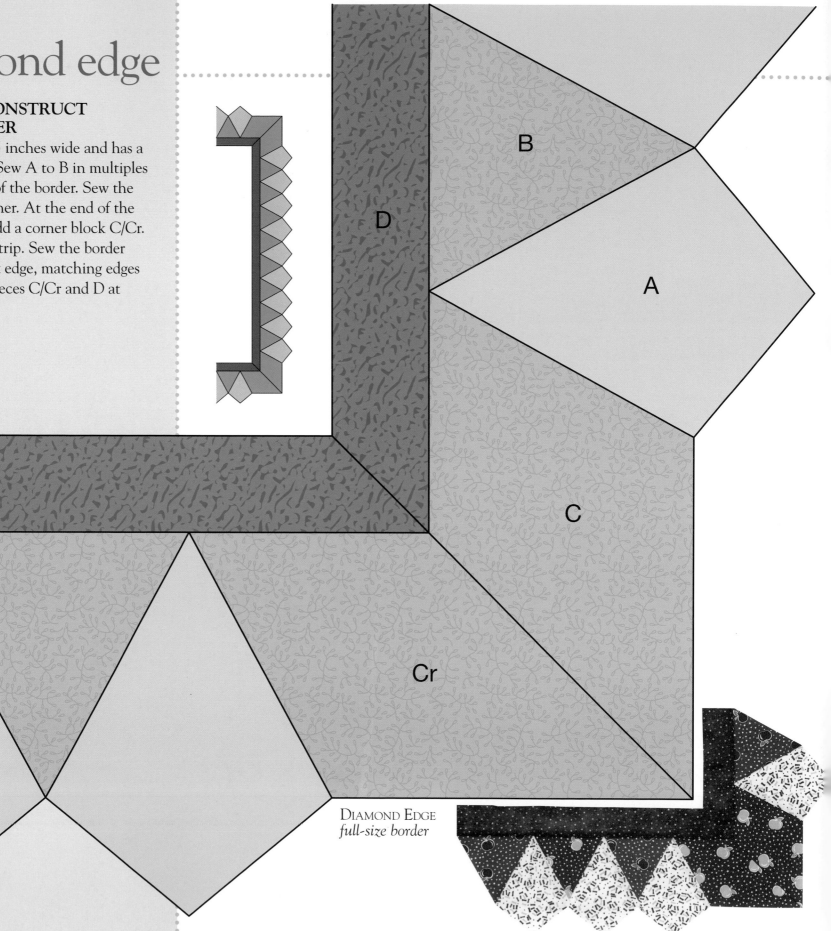

DIAMOND EDGE
full-size border

CHECKERBOARD *full-size border*

checkerboard

HOW TO CONSTRUCT THIS BORDER

For one 6-inch-square unit, sew six A pieces together to form a row. Sew a 6-inch-long B piece (or extend to desired length to fit quilt) to A unit. For the corner, sew two A pieces together. Join AA unit to C piece. Sew three A pieces together. Join AAA unit to the AAC unit to form a square. Sew the square corner unit to AAAAAAB unit.

quilting basics

HOW TO MAKE PIECED-BLOCK TEMPLATES

All of our patterns are finished-size to make creating your templates easy and frustration-free. When selecting your template plastic, choose the kind of plastic that is slightly frosted. You can still see through it, spot it easily, and mark on it without smearing or smudging. For the blocks in this book, steer away from template plastic with a grid printed on it. Avoid using cardboard for templates; it doesn't hold its shape well with continuous use.

Using a ruler and a fine-line permanent marker, trace the block pattern pieces onto your plastic. You'll add the ¼-inch seam allowance when you cut out the pieces. (See information below for making appliqué templates.) Then cut out using scissors. It is not necessary to move the template plastic when tracing each template. If several pieces are grouped together, draw them that way, then cut them apart.

Note that we have labeled our block patterns using letters of the alphabet. Label your templates with these same letters using a permanent marker. Remember, the letters in each block are for that block only; piece B in one block isn't the same as B used in another block.

In some of the block patterns you will see pieces marked with a letter followed by a lowercase "r" (as in B and Br). This means that you must reverse (flip over) the B template to trace and cut this piece. You don't need two templates to cut B and Br: You simply use the other side of your B template. Instructions for making the blocks will often include a direction such as "(4 times)." This means that you create the unit described a total of four times. As you draw the templates, note any edge that will be on the outside of the block. Mark the template with an arrow along this edge to remind you to cut the fabric with the arrow on the straight of the grain. This will help keep your block from stretching. Also mark which edges are to be sewn together.

To store your blocks, small, clear plastic bags help keep each of your block templates separate and easy to find. These easy-to-label zipper-lock bags are available at quilting and craft stores.

HOW TO MAKE APPLIQUÉ-BLOCK TEMPLATES

Trace the entire design onto template plastic, as described above. Letter the pieces in the design, and also letter the corresponding pieces on the template plastic. Then cut out the individual template pieces.

Trace around the template pieces on the right side of the fabric with the template face up. Make a dotted line on the template to indicate areas that will be lying under another shape.

TRANSFERRING THE PATTERN FROM TEMPLATE TO FABRIC

Before you do any tracing and cutting of the fabric, you must decide if your quilting project will ever need to be washed. If so, you must prewash the fabric. If the fabric

is going to shrink, or the dyes are going to run, you want it to happen before you stitch.

Lay your fabric out smoothly, wrong side up. Try using elements of the fabric print to enhance the design of the block, centering a flower or stripe for instance.

Position the template facedown on the wrong side of the fabric. It is a good practice to always place the template facedown on the fabric, even when it doesn't seem to matter. There are times when it is very important, and this habit will help you avoid redrawing.

For appliquéd blocks, mark fabric on the right side. The seam allowance (between ⅛ and ¼ inch) is added when you cut out each piece.

Trace around the template onto the fabric using a No. 2 pencil. This is the line on which you will sew. Mechanical pencils are excellent, because they stay sharp. Don't choose one with lead that is too thin—the 0.7mm size is small enough. If using dark fabrics, choose colored leads.

For pieced blocks, add a ¼-inch seam allowance to all sides using a ruler. You'll need a clear ruler printed with a fine-line ⅛-inch grid. Many of these rulers are not 100 percent accurate—the ¼-inch mark may be different on opposite sides of the ruler. If you own one of these, choose one edge and use only that edge.

Transfer the template marks indicating which edges are to be sewn together to the seam allowances of the fabric. This is especially helpful when, for instance, a triangle has two sides of similar length.

HOW TO MAKE PIECED BLOCKS

Use your fabric scissors to cut out your fabric pieces along the seam allowance lines. When the pieces are all cut out, refer to our easy-to-follow instructions for the sequence in putting your block together.

As you begin to feed the pieces into your sewing machine, it is not necessary to backstitch; you will be sewing over the ends of the seams, so they aren't in danger of coming unsewn. Also, if you make a mistake, it is easier to rip out a seam that is not backstitched.

As each seam is pieced, you may want to trim away some of the points that protrude beyond the end of the seam allowance. Some of the seams may also need to be trimmed if they will be caught in the next seam you will sew.

HOW TO MAKE FOUR- AND NINE-PATCH BLOCKS

A Four-Patch and a Nine-Patch are two common types of pieced blocks. A Four-Patch is a square made of four smaller squares. To assemble, sew two together two times (making two pairs of squares); then join the two pairs into a square. A Nine-Patch is a square made up of nine smaller squares-three rows of three squares each. To make a nine-patch, sew three squares together in a row three times, making three rows; then sew the rows together to make the larger square.

HOW TO MAKE APPLIQUÉD BLOCKS

There are several ways to do appliqué. We turn the edges of our pieces under with the needle as we sew. Basting beforehand is another option. Be sure to never use a colored thread if using the basting method. A contrasting thread can leave little, unsightly dots of color on the fabric.

Concave (inward) curves should be clipped before basting. Clip around the curve only up to ¹⁄₁₆ inch from the seam line. (If you clip right up to the line, you will get points along the curve.)

To baste each piece, roll the seam edge under along the marked line. Do not turn under seams that will lie under another shape, as this produces bulky ridges on the finished surface.

The actual application of one fabric piece to another is done with blindstitching. Using thread that matches the piece being applied, bring your needle from the back to the front, catching a few threads of the rolled edge. Pull thread through. Re-enter the base fabric at the exact spot and slightly under the rolled edge. Make a linear stitch on the back, following the outline of the shape, coming up again through all layers. The linear stitches should be not more than ⅛ inch in length, less for very small or intricately shaped pieces.

When all application is finished, remove basting threads. Any embroidery can then be added.

HOW TO MAKE FUSED-APPLIQUÉ BLOCKS

As an alternate method of appliqué, trace each pattern piece onto fusing-adhesive material. Cut out the pieces and fuse to the wrong side of the chosen fabrics. Cut out and remove the paper. On a 10-inch background square, arrange each piece as the instructions specify and press in place. Use a machine satin stitch or hand embroider the edges of the fused pieces. Trim the block to measure 9½ inches square.

ACCENT STITCHES

For detail accents, specialty stitches are often added to a completed quilt block. You'll see these stitches are represented by dashed lines on the block patterns. The illustrations, right, will help you master the common stitches which we have also used in this book.

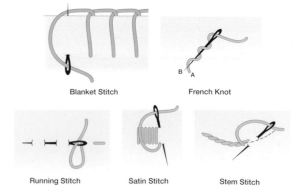

Blanket Stitch French Knot

Running Stitch Satin Stitch Stem Stitch

STRIP PIECING

In traditional patchwork, pieces are marked, cut, and sewn together one piece at a time. But when squares and rectangles are combined in a repeated pattern, you can simplify assembly by using strip-piecing techniques.

Cutting Strips

With strip piecing, you sew together a specified sequence of horizontal strips into a strip set. The strip set is then cut into vertical units, each of which represents a row or unit of a quilt block.

Strips are cut on the crosswise grain, ½ inch wider than the desired finished size of the patch to allow for ¼-inch seam allowances. For example, for a 2-inch finished square, cut a strip 2½ inches wide.

Strip Sets

By cutting units different widths or turning them upside down, a strip set is often used for more than one block row.

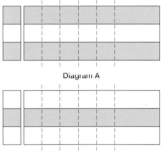

Diagram A

Diagram B

DESIGNING THE QUILT

When determining how big you want to make your quilt, how to join your blocks together, and what border to choose, be sure to do your calculations carefully.

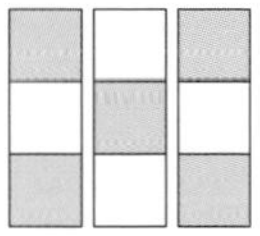

Diagram C

While there is no one "standard" quilt dimension for any size of bed, we can give you some guidelines to follow when planning your bed quilt. Here's a chart to help you decide what size of quilt you want to make:

width ranges		length ranges	
twin	full	twin	full
63"-81"	78"-96"	87"-106"	87"-106"
queen	king	queen	king
84"-102"	100"-118"	92"-112"	92"-112"

Sashing

Fabric strips that separate or frame the blocks are called sashing strips. They enhance a quilt design and enlarge the quilt center.

Adjusting the width of the sashing strips is one way to make your quilt larger or smaller. Other ways to alter the finished size of your quilt include:
- Use more or fewer quilt blocks.
- Add or delete sashing strips.
- Select a wider or narrower border.
- Change the layout of the blocks or add setting blocks.

Finishing the Border

Most quilters prefer to use binding when finishing the border edges of a quilt. However, you can use a blind-hem stitch or face the quilt, if desired.

BACKING AND BINDING

To back a quilt, you simply cut a piece of the fabric you have chosen, making it at least 3 inches larger on all sides than the quilt top. (The larger the quilt, and the more quilting you plan to do, the more extra fabric you should allow on all sides.) If the quilt is larger than the fabric you want to use, you will have to piece the backing to make it the right size. Layer the top, batting, and backing, with wrong sides of the top and backing toward the batting. Baste the layers together and quilt as desired.

How to Bind the Quilt

Choose ¼- or ½-inch binding and cut as described above (and long enough to go all the way around the quilt with a few inches to spare).

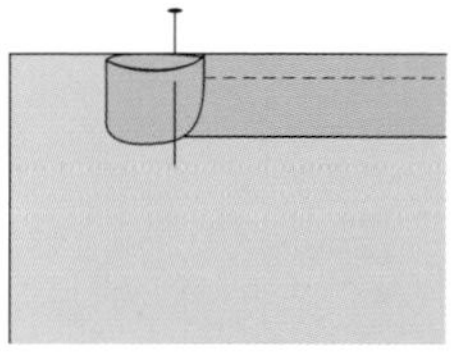

Quarter-Inch Binding

Cut binding 2 inches wide. Use ¼-inch seam allowances.

Half-Inch Binding

Cut binding 2½ inches wide. Use ¼-inch seam allowances.

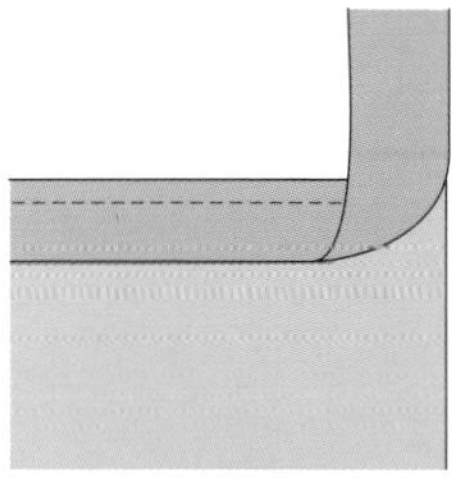

Diagram 1

Piece the binding as necessary using a diagonal joining seam to reach the required length, pressing seams open. Then press the binding in half (wrong sides together) along the length. Lay binding along the raw edge of the quilt, folding over the beginning binding edge, right before stitching (see Diagram 1). Stitch, using the correct seam allowance.

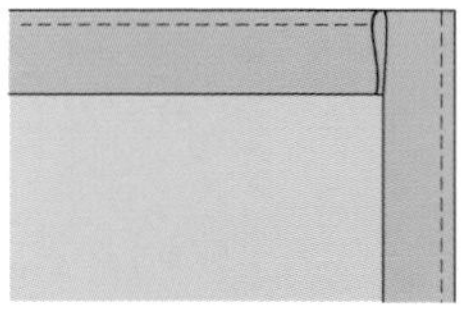

Diagram 2

Stop stitching ¼ inch from the corner. Backstitch and break the thread. Fold binding up, as shown in Diagram 2, then down (see Diagram 3), and stitch from edge. Repeat the process at each corner of the quilt. When you return to the starting point, over-lap the end of the binding strip beyond the fold in the first end. Trim the backing and batting even with the edge of the quilt front. Turn binding up and over the edge to the back of the quilt. Tuck binding in at corners on back to make a miter. Hand-stitch the binding to the backing, being careful not to sew through to the front.

Diagram 3

Select a Batting

A variety of choices are available in batting fiber content, loft, warmth, ease of needling, softness, and washability. The qualities of the batting you use should complement the nature and future use of your quilt.

Cut Bias Strips

To cut bias strips, begin with a fabric square or rectangle. Use a large acrylic triangle to square

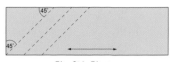

Bias Strip Diagram

up the left edge of the fabric and to draw lines at a 45° angle (see Bias Strip Diagram). Cut the fabric on the drawn lines. Handle the edges carefully to avoid distorting the bias. Cut enough strips to total the length needed. Join the strips with diagonal seams to make one continuous binding strip.

Make Mitered Border Corners

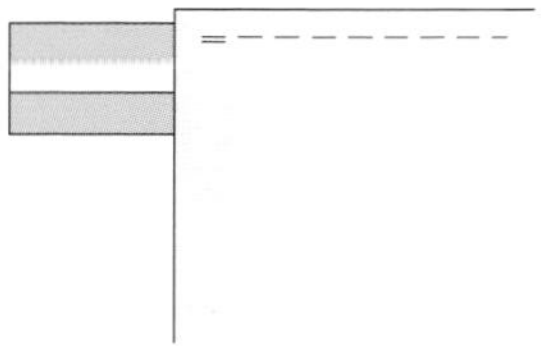

Pin a border strip to one edge of the quilt top, matching the center of the strip to the center of the quilt top edge. Sew together, beginning and ending the seam ¼ inch from the edge of the quilt top (see Diagram A, right). Allow excess border fabric to extend beyond each edge. Repeat with remaining border strips. Press the seam allowances toward the border strips.

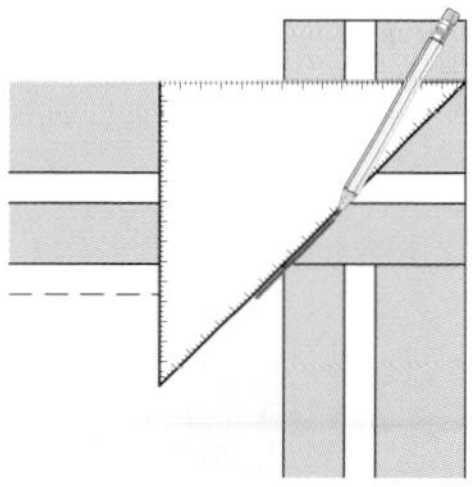

Diagram A

Overlap the border strips at each corner (see Diagram B, right). Align the edge of a top border. With a pencil, draw along the edge of the triangle from the border seam to the outside corner. Place the bottom border on top and repeat marking process.

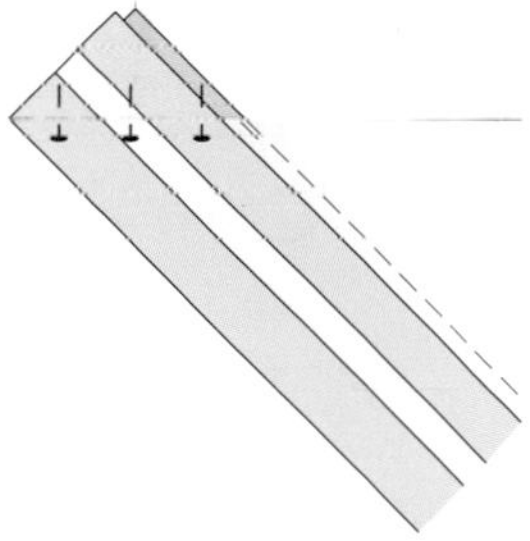

Diagram B

With the right sides of adjacent border strips together, match the marked seam lines and pin (see Diagram C, right). Beginning with a backstitch at the inside corner, stitch exactly on the marked lines to the outside edge of the borders. Check the right side of the corner to see that it lies flat. Then trim the excess fabric, leaving a ¼-inch seam allowance. Press the seam open. Mark and sew remaining corners in this manner.

Diagram C

Prairie Points

To make prairie points, cut fabric squares as indicated in instructions. Press squares in half

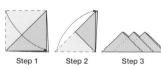

Step 1   Step 2   Step 3

diagonally twice, right side out. Using the steps, above, pin the triangles evenly along the edges of the project front with all of the double-folds facing the same direction. Lap adjacent edges, or slip single-folds inside double-folds. Stitch on seam line.

index, sources & resources

Amish Cross.....168
Amish Shadows.....186
Anvil.....124
Autumn Star.....36
Basket Variation.....132
Basket Weave.....136
Butterfly.....152
Card Tricks.....194
Carolina Liy.....82
Checkerboard Border.....213
Color Triangle.....166
Colorado Block.....200
Cornucopia.....70
Country Decision.....158
Country Boy.....142
Country Pinwheel.....172
Crazy Ann.....154
Criss Cross.....196
Crossroads.....122
Delectable Mountains.....198
Diamond & Stripes Border.....206
Diamond Edge Border.....212
Diamond Five.....118
Diamond Link Border.....211
Dimensional Star.....10
Dogwood.....104

Dresden Plate.....150
Drunkard's Path.....138
Eclectic Border.....207
Eight Pointed Star.....38
Embroidered Basket.....62
Fan Blades.....134
Fan Border.....210
Feathered Star.....48
Fireworks.....52
Floral Appliqué.....60
Floral Fancies.....80
Floral Heart.....20
Floral Sunburst.....66
Flower Basket.....72
Flower in the Window.....100
Flowers Four.....102
Fool's Puzzle.....146
Four Hearts.....30
Four Stars.....26
Four-pointed Checkered Star.....28
Garden Flower.....92
Geese in the Corner.....110
Geometric Butterfly.....174
Geometric Star.....24
Geometry.....190
Goose Tracks.....144

Heart Patches.....44
Hearts and Gizzards.....130
Hugs and Kisses.....184
Irish Chain.....204
Jacob's Ladder Variation.....112
Jewel Star.....178
King's Crown.....180
Log Cabin.....148
Lone Star.....22
Mariner's Compass.....16
Martha's Vineyard.....78
Middle Ground.....170
Mosaic Star.....12
Ohio Rose.....74
Pansies.....68
Peony.....76
Pinwheel.....156
Poppies.....86
Posy Row.....96
Prairie Point Flower.....90
Prairie Queen.....120
Pretty Bow.....126
Rainbow Stars.....46
Rectangle Makes the Square.....164
Rotating Star.....40
Sawtooth.....202

Sawtooth Border.....209
Shoo Fly.....128
Silk Stars.....8
Spiced Pinks.....88
Squares in the Corner.....114
Star Fan.....14
Star Shades.....50
Stars and Hearts.....42
Streak of Lightning.....188
Sunbonnet with Purse.....140
Texas Tulip.....64
Tile Heart.....54
Tipsy Star.....18
Tree of Life.....116
Triangles Border.....208
Twisted Star.....32
Tulip.....84
Tulip Bouquet.....94
Turkey Tracks Variation.....182
Two Star.....34
Waves.....192
Wild Rose.....98
Woven Ribbon.....176

SOURCES

BALIFABRICS-PRINCESS MIRAH DESIGN
(800) 783-4612
BATIK@BALIFAB.COM
www.balifab.com

BENATEX, INC.
1359 Broadway, Suite 1100
New York, NY 10018
(212) 840-3250
www.benartex.com

CRANSTON PRINTWORKS CO.
2 Worcester Road
Webster, MA 01570
www.QuiltingTreasures.com

DAN RIVER, INC.
1065 Avenue of Americas
New York, NY 10018
(434) 799-7000

FABRI-QUILT, INC.
901 E. 14th Ave.
North Kansas City, MO 64116
(816) 421-2000

MARCUS BROTHERS TEXTILES, INC.
980 Avenue of the America's
New York, NY 10018
(212) 354-8700
www.marcusbrothers.com

P & B TEXTILES
1580 Gilbreth Road
Burlingame, CA 94010-1605
(650) 692-0422
www.pbtex.com

HENRY GLASS & CO., INC.
49 West 37th Street
New York, NY 10018
(212) 686-5194

RJR FASHION FABRICS
2203 Dominquez Street
Building K-3
Torrance CA 90501
(800) 422-5426

ROBERT KAUFMAN CO., INC.
135 W. 132nd St.
Los Angeles, CA 90061
(310) 538-3482

V.I.P. FABRICS
1412 Broadway
New York, NY 10018
(800) 847-4064

A special thanks to Ardith Field for sharing many of her quilts and antique items shown in this book.

RESOURCES

American Patchwork and Quilting, Better Homes and Gardens Books, 1985

Better Homes and Gardens American Patchwork and Quilting magazine

Better Homes and Gardens America's Heritage Quilts, Meredith Press, 1991

Complete Guide to Quilting, Audrey Heard and Beverly Pryor, Creative Home Library in association with Meredith, 1974

The Amish Quilt, Eve Wheatcroft Granick, Good Books, 1994

The Romance of the Patchwork Quilt in America, Carrie Hall and Rose Kretsinger, Bonanza Books, 1935

www.Quiltstudy.org

www.Womenfolk.com